Lessons in Loss

Lessons in Loss

*What Every Therapist
Needs to Know*

Ginny Pizzardi, M.S., M.F.T.

YANA PRESS

Copyright © 2011 by Ginny Pizzardi

All rights reserved. No part of this book may be used or reproduced in any manner whatsoever without written permission except in the case of brief quotations embodied in critical articles and reviews.

Contact the author directly for further information or permissions:
www.GinnyPizzardi.com
(415) 285-4061

Published by
YANA PRESS
www.YanaPress.com

To my beloved daughter, Emma,

whom I love and respect

more than words can say.

TABLE OF CONTENTS

Acknowledgements   ix

Introduction   xi

PART ONE
Loss: Why Does It Matter?

CHAPTER ONE   3
    The Impact of Unresolved Loss

CHAPTER TWO   13
    The Unconscious Mind – Why Unresolved
    Loss Is So Powerful

CHAPTER THREE   23
    Unearthing Past Experiences of Loss

PART TWO
Your Client's Experience

CHAPTER FOUR   37
    When Safety, Self-Worth, and Boundaries Are
    Violated: *Physical & Sexual Abuse, Emotional*
    Abuse & Neglect, Domestic Violence

CHAPTER FIVE 55
   When the Family Unit Is Broken: *Divorce and Adoption*

CHAPTER SIX 73
   When Physical or Emotional Health is Disrupted: *Death & Mortality, Illness & Injury, Addiction & Recovery*

CHAPTER SEVEN 97
   The Many Faces of Loss: *Loss of a Job, Life Changes, Trauma, and More*

PART THREE
The Solutions

CHAPTER EIGHT 109
   Treatment Strategies for Healing Unresolved Loss

CHAPTER NINE 135
   A Therapist's Blind Spots

CHAPTER TEN 143
   Healing the Healer

About the Author 149

Acknowledgements

I offer my deepest gratitude to my editor, Jan Allegretti, who is not only an excellent writer and editor, but whose patience, enthusiasm, wonderful input, and kindness were limitless. I also want to thank Hal Bennett, whose mentorship and trust in the human spirit helped me move forward to complete this book.

My heartfelt thanks to Karen Peoples, a constant source of guidance and inspiration. She has been the light on my path through unspeakable loss, and helped me discover how to turn loss into an emotional, spiritual, and intellectual awakening.

A very special thanks to the following people who believed in this project and helped make it happen: my dear friend Gregory Vogel, whose advice, expertise, and "tough love" have been a blessing throughout my life and at various stages of this production; my friend Jon Rendell for his generosity of time, talent, humor, and consultation on the graphics.

I have many friends and colleagues to thank for their constant support, encouragement, and friendship, but especially my loving family of friends: Teri Abramsky, for your life-long love, friendship, and unwavering belief in me; Lynda Fassino, Cindy Halvorson, Eileen Levy; Ellen Litman; Scott Madover; Jack Morin, Nan O'Connor, Saralie Pennington, Jean Siciliano, Lisa Szer, and Mikael Wagner.

Finally, I want to acknowledge all of the children, adolescents, women, and men who can't be mentioned by name, who let me join them on their courageous journey to heal.

Introduction

I've been a psychotherapist for more than twenty-six years. I have derived great satisfaction and fulfillment from my work, while learning more than I ever dreamed I could about the human heart and soul. More importantly, like you, I've lived a life rich with joy and heartache, success and failure, loving and letting go. Through it all I've discovered that virtually every life experience carries an element of loss. Some of those losses give us a chance to celebrate the end of an old chapter and the beginning of something new. At other times the losses tear our hearts to shreds. What we do with that pain determines the course of our lives for years to come, and our ability to embrace all that life has to offer.

To live is to lose. Our infinite stories of loss start early, persist through every change and passage, and define our endings. It starts the day we enter this world; birth is actually the loss of the safest and most protected state we will ever experience, yet we tend to ignore or misunderstand this elemental fact. And so, we begin our journey on this planet with a loss we never name, acknowledge, or grieve. By the time we grow up, most of us have acquired years of cumulative loss that has never been acknowledged, let alone resolved. I've come to believe that this single lapse is at the root of much of the suffering we see around us—in individuals and in the world at large.

We live in a society that underestimates the impact our losses have on our emotional, psychological, physical and spiritual lives. Our cultural fear of raw emotions is so deeply ingrained that, from an early age, most of us have been taught to stop crying, get over it, quit being so self-involved. We learn to bury those feelings deep in our unconscious, where they become gatekeepers of a silent prison. We remain isolated and alone, unable to connect deeply with ourselves or others, incapable of experiencing the sorrow or joy that makes life worthwhile.

How might our relationships with each other—and the vitality of our society as a whole—be different if we could be spontaneous and truthful about our losses and the emotions that attend them? If we can get in touch with our most closely held feelings, express ourselves to someone who cares, and embrace all that those emotions have to teach us, we can become free again to experience true connection with ourselves and with those around us.

That's where you come in. You're in the unique position of one who can help open the doors to freedom, and cast a light of understanding on the dark mystery of unresolved loss. As you walk side by side with each client on the difficult, often painful, but lifesaving journey to rediscover the losses that were never acknowledged, you'll help her find the emotional freedom necessary to live the life she was meant to live.

Of course, psychotherapy is not only about resolving loss. It is a complicated process that involves helping people to understand themselves, to gain awareness of their conscious and unconscious wishes, and to recognize their many strengths, fears, challenges, and limitations. However, I propose that loss is a part of every problem we—and our clients—face. Although each of us is unique and each of us responds differently to similar life experiences, we all share common emotional reactions. A central focus of our work as therapists is to help each individual learn to identify and express her emotional life in ways that will facilitate her connection with herself and her connection to others. An understanding of the losses she has endured, and an ability to experience and release the emotions associated with those losses, is essential to her ability to connect in deep and lasting ways.

Nature has given us the capacity to withstand our losses, to grow larger and stronger through them—and even to transcend them. As therapists, we are but Nature's teachers, with the opportunity to guide each client on her own journey of transcendence. As George Bernard Shaw has said,

Life is no brief candle to me. It is a sort of splendid torch which I have got hold of for the moment, and I want to make it burn as brightly as possible before handing it on to future generations.

With this book, I pass my own torch of understanding on to you. May it help to light your path, and that of every client who is fortunate enough to have you as her guide.

PART ONE

**Loss:
Why Does It Matter?**

CHAPTER ONE

The Impact of Unresolved Loss

You've become a therapist because you want to help. Day after day you see clients struggling with one issue or another, to one degree or another. In some cases you deftly help them move through their crises and move on with their lives, and you rest easy knowing you provided the treatment they needed.

But then there are the others...the ones who just never seem to get better, or who do improve but then return months later with new crises that seem eerily similar to the ones you helped them solve the first time around. Why is it so hard to make a difference with clients like these? Are they fundamentally flawed somehow, with no hope of ever being happy? Are there some clues lurking within their stories that might tell you what's standing between them and the rich, rewarding lives they long for?

Sometimes it seems that if you could just find the right questions to ask, or if you just knew where to look in their files to find the key to their struggles, you'd be able to help them turn the corner toward deeper, lasting healing. But what are the right questions? Where should you look?

The good news is that you're holding answers to all those questions right here in your hands. In the pages that follow we'll explore the single most common reason your clients are unhappy or unfulfilled or lonely—or whatever the reasons are they're seeking your help. Most important, you'll discover how you can guide them through the process of discovery and healing that will lead to the lasting healing that you—and they—desire.

It may come as a surprise that one small book can provide an important key to treating everyone who walks through your doors. After all, no two clients are the same. It's true, of course, that every client you see is unique, with a history and profile unlike any other. But there are three things that all of them have in common:

- Each has a desire to be happy, to love and be loved, to enjoy success.
- Something in his or her life—relationships, career, finances, or perhaps emotional equilibrium—is not working out as it should.
- Each has experienced loss of one kind or another.

That last item on the list, the experience of loss, is the missing piece of the puzzle that you've been looking for. As you develop your understanding of how loss is related to the first two items on the list, you'll discover the roots of your clients' suffering and an essential key to helping them heal more quickly and completely. That's what this book is all about.

What Do We Mean by "Loss"?

Let's begin by exploring exactly what loss is, and the many forms it can take. By definition, *loss is simply the experience of no longer having someone or something that was valued.* Who or what is that "someone or something"? Initially we tend to think of tangibles, such as a loved one or financial assets. But as you know, there are many things we value that are less easily identified, such as trust, dignity, a sense of self-worth, or the belief that the world is a safe place to be. Clearly, the loss of any of these intangibles will have a profound impact on the life of a client.

As you can see, our definition of "loss" can apply to a broad range of life experiences—and it's clear that none of us is immune. From a very early age each of us experiences loss of different kinds and degrees, and it's a frequent visitor throughout our lives. Most any experience that brings unhappiness, fear, or physical or emotional trauma includes an element of loss. Let's look at some examples.

Death

Death is the ultimate separation, and a form of loss everyone can understand. When someone we love dies we are left with an empty space in our hearts, our homes, our lives. Often there is pronounced emotional pain, and even a physical sensation of pain in the heart, stomach, or elsewhere in the body.

> *Barbara's mom got TB and died when she was eleven. Her dad sold their big Victorian house and took a job traveling, leaving the kids with their tight-lipped Old World grandmother, who taught her that crying was a sign of weakness. As the painful memories of her mother's death began to fade, Barbara was left wondering why a part of her seemed to be missing.*

Divorce

Parental divorce or separation can leave a child with a permanent sense of abandonment, with devastating effects. When an adult experiences divorce, feelings of abandonment, the loss of a dream, and loss of self-esteem are common.

> *Jim's mom didn't die. She suffered from depression for years, and when Jim was eleven years old she simply walked away from their "picture-perfect" suburban life and never came back. Eventually his dad filed for divorce. But from the time his mother left, Jim had real trouble connecting with people, and developed the habit of keeping a polite distance from almost everyone.*

Physical and sexual abuse

Physical and sexual abuse leave the victim with a loss of trust, a loss of dignity, and a loss of self-esteem.

> *Monica's father was a charming man who had an ugly side that surfaced whenever he drank. Even as small children, Monica and her brothers were often awakened in the middle of the night to "play," which was really an excuse for him to harangue them with his frustrations or knock them around. It's not surprising*

that Monica married Ted, a handsome young alcoholic, because he "felt like family."

Emotional abuse, shaming, and criticism

This type of abuse may be the most common, and is surprisingly widespread. It happens in the classroom, on the job, among friends, and around the dinner table.

Micah grew up in a twisted world of guilt. At the dinner table his mother would ask, "Would you like peas or carrots?" If he chose peas, she'd ask, "Why don't you like my carrots?" As if the guilt wasn't enough, there was a sense of shame in the family that seemed to get passed from one generation to the next. Although Micah was bright, hard working, and generous, he carried this psychic burden of shame with him wherever he went.

Neglect and emotional distance

When parents are absent—or when they're simply not *emotionally* present—often the child's physical, nutritional, or emotional needs are not met. Kids lose their sense of trust and safety, and their sense of self-worth is often damaged or lost.

Sara grew up in a house with two hard-working parents, but they were never home. When they were, they seemed to spend most of their time arguing with each other or criticizing her. Neither parent really knew what a family was or how to create one, having never experienced a real family themselves. As an only child, Sara was often the target of their anxiety and frustrations.

These examples are just a brief sampling of the kinds of issues your clients may be dealing with. Every life has its own challenges—every family and every generation within the family suffers loss in one form or another. War, death, trauma, infidelity, divorce, abuse, rape, immigration, isolation, poverty, bankruptcy, estrangement, detachment—who can say which losses are harder to live with. What's important is to recognize the profound and lasting impact they can have when they are not acknowledged, and the emotions that go with them remain unspoken and unresolved.

The Symptoms of Unresolved Loss

How will you know if your client is dealing with unresolved loss? What should you look for?

The quick and easy answer is this: If she is sitting in your office, chances are she's dealing with unresolved loss. In the vast majority of cases, any inability to function well can be traced to a past incidence of loss that has not been adequately dealt with. It's safe to assume that the issue that caused your client to contact you for help is no exception. If the treatment plan you've been following has not been successful, it's a good sign you'll need to dig a little deeper to find the trauma that is the real root of the problem.

There are some common coping strategies individuals use to ease the pain of unresolved loss, or the inadequacies they carry because of them. When you see those coping strategies in a client, it's a signal that he needs your help to uncover the pain he's trying to mask. The following are just a few examples.

Addictions — they're not just about drugs

Many people live with constant anxiety or emotional pain just below the surface. If the discomfort is always there, anything that makes it go away for a few hours is welcome. There's a wide variety of distractions to choose from, and any of those can be abused—that is, used to excess—or even become an addiction. Alcohol, drugs, and cigarettes are the ones that typically come to mind. But even things we usually think of as normal and healthy, such as food, sex, work, shopping, or even television and video games, can be used to excess. In recent years the fitness craze has even inspired some individuals to use working out as their drug of choice.

Much like a drug, any of these activities has the capacity to numb the pain and provide an escape. If your client engages in any of them to the extent that they interfere with the more positive components of life, or with her ability to maintain a healthy balance between the various aspects of her life, it qualifies as abuse or, quite possibly, an addiction. And there's a good chance that addiction is her way of shielding herself from the pain of unresolved loss.

Underachievement

Often someone who has experienced emotional abuse suffers from a fear of failure or fear of success. They may spend years in careers that don't utilize their training or talents, sabotage opportunities that come their way, or otherwise fail to live up to their potential.

As a youngster Jeannie was constantly nagged by her dad, admonished that she "wasn't living up to her potential," no matter how much she actually did accomplish—which in her case was a lot. When I met Jeannie she was an attorney in a law firm that advocated for environmental issues. She shared with me that the firm's law partners had been asking her to become a partner for the previous couple of years. She confessed that she was terrified of taking on that responsibility because she believed she didn't "have what it takes," and that her prior successes at the firm were due to "good luck" and cases that were poorly brought by the plaintiffs.

Difficult relationships

When life experiences have been overwhelming, many people become emotionally isolated. It becomes more and more difficult to be intimate or to have satisfying relationships. Often they have trouble tuning in to the needs of the people they love or work with. They may isolate themselves physically, spending most of their time alone. Others may form relationships but avoid deep commitment, depriving themselves of the passion and connection they crave. Some seek solace in a fantasy world of movies, novels, or pornography.

Mark was a handsomely rugged man in his late forties, who liked living "close to the land." He made a good living, and had built himself a beautiful home up in the mountains, a forty-minute drive from the nearest town. He'd been married once for two years, and had one other serious relationship that lasted about eighteen months. He told me he longed for someone to share his life with, but just couldn't find a woman he could relate to. In the meantime, he said, he was content to "just hang with the coyotes and the hawks and the redwood trees."

How You Can Help

Awareness is the first step toward change—for you and, of course, for your clients. As you become more aware of the powerful role unresolved loss plays in the struggles your clients face today, you'll be better equipped to help them become aware of the emotional pain that prevents them from living the lives they were meant to live.

In the coming chapters you'll discover why the feelings associated with loss so often remain hidden, and why they're so powerful when they do. You'll gain an understanding of the many different types of loss, and the impact each can have in the adult lives of the clients you see. You'll also learn simple techniques you can use in your treatment plans to guide your clients through the process of uncovering unresolved loss and releasing those old hidden emotions. Finally, you'll become acquainted with the ways your own experience of loss may be affecting your ability to treat your clients successfully—and how you can heal your own wounds as well.

What's most important is that you've taken the first step toward gaining the awareness you need to become the most effective therapist you can be. With this book as your guide, you as well as your clients will discover a whole new world of understanding, success, and fulfillment in your work and in every aspect of your lives.

CHAPTER TWO

The Unconscious Mind – Why Unresolved Loss Is So Powerful

It's clear that everyone experiences loss, to varying degrees, time and time again. It's an inevitable part of life. Why, then, does it play such an important role in mental illness and therapy? If loss is an inevitable part of life, wouldn't it seem that we'd all be able to handle it with ease, and just roll with the punches and move on?

We can—but only if we're able to be fully present with the experience and all the emotions that go with it. Unfortunately, this is rarely the case. Too often the feelings barely register on our radar. In fact, many of us tend to put a lot of effort and energy into *not* feeling the feelings. And that's where we get into trouble.

As a therapist, it's essential to keep in mind that even when a client represses his emotions, so that they're no longer part of his conscious awareness, they're never completely gone from the deeper reaches of his mind. Emotions that remain unresolved, and left to stew in the *unconscious* mind, can exert a powerful impact on his choices, his actions, and his quality of life.

Running from the truth

Chances are you know what it's like to avoid feeling painful emotions. You go through a difficult breakup, a beloved companion dies, or you're passed over for that promotion you were hoping for, and you find yourself using food or shopping or television or work as a distraction. You might make a conscious choice to keep yourself busy to avoid "wallowing in your sadness." Or maybe you simply notice one day that you're exhausted, as though you've been running a marathon, and suddenly you realize you've been unwittingly running away from your heartache. Either way, you've successfully kept the pain buried somewhere inside, beyond the reach of your awareness.

You've probably seen something similar going on from time to time with your clients. In some cases they know they've been through a difficult experience but are reluctant to acknowledge how painful it really was, or they're convinced they've suffered enough and want to move on. Other individuals are completely unaware that a particular event bothered them as much as it really did. Still others have experienced trauma so severe it's been completely blocked from their conscious memory.

Any one of these scenarios can severely undermine a client's ability to function. Understanding why this is true, and the various ways emotions become buried within the psyche, will enable you to help peel away the layers of avoidance so that emotions flow more freely, and the individuals who come to you for help find their way to greater emotional freedom and happiness.

Losses we never mourned

For most of us, repressing our feelings isn't a habit we develop as adults. It's a pattern that started when we were small children—an essential one, really, that was necessary to get us through childhood. When we're kids, we're totally dependent on our families for survival, physically and emotionally. We need our parents to feed us, shelter us, protect us from danger, and give us the love and nurturing that are necessary for us to thrive. But as children we're not in control of how things go—and if they don't go well, usually we can't leave. If we don't get the care we need, if we're treated badly, or if life simply brings its inevitable lumps and bumps, we have to find a way to cope with the loss. As infants we don't have the mental capacity to understand the actions of others—we just know that we hurt, or we're hungry, lonely, or otherwise unhappy. As older children we may cognitively understand what's going on, but lack the emotional maturity or skills to process it. Either way, the mind responds by repressing those negative emotions. We may even repress the event itself, and have no conscious memory that it happened at all.

When adults experience loss, we're more likely to retain an awareness of the event and the fact that it was difficult to endure. But for a variety of reasons we often don't allow ourselves to feel or express the emotions associated with it. For one thing, most people retain the pattern of repression that started in childhood. For another, in our culture it's often not considered appropriate or acceptable to wear our emotions on our sleeves. Society tends to reward strength and stoicism more than sensitivity, so there's added pressure to pretend everything's okay even when it's not. As a part of that norm, many people never develop the skills to process emotions in a healthy way.

When repression is very strong, the process may go beyond *pretending* that everything is okay—we may actually believe it. The pain of loss may be so thoroughly buried that we don't even know we hurt, or we may hurt or feel depressed but have no idea why.

Where did all the feelings go?

If we have no awareness of painful emotions, or even of the events that triggered them, it might seem logical that we'd be free of them. Nothing could be further from the truth. For children and adults alike, the memory of loss stays within us, buried beyond conscious awareness deep in the unconscious mind. As long as it remains there, the fear or sadness you experienced as a child is still a part of your psyche, even if you don't remember the emotion or the event that triggered it. Similarly, when a tragic event occurs during adulthood, if the heartache or grief is not fully experienced and resolved it will fester in your unconscious mind and undermine your ability to function at your best—even if you've convinced yourself it really wasn't so bad.

Emotions that are buried in the unconscious have a particularly powerful impact on our lives. When they're beyond our awareness they're also beyond our understanding and control. They operate like a sinister puppeteer lurking behind a dark curtain, pulling the strings of our psyche so that our emotions, our choices, and our actions dance across the stage in ways we often cannot understand. Our relationships, our success on the job, the choices we make, our ability to experience joy as well as sorrow, and much more will suffer. New losses, even if they're relatively minor ones, can generate a flood of emotion because they trigger the pent-up response to a similar loss that occurred long ago. Losses that occurred during childhood can virtually rule our lives forever if we are not able to revisit them and resolve the emotions they carry.

A therapist's approach to the unconscious mind

Many of the difficulties that bring clients into your office are rooted in emotions buried in the unconscious mind. Depression, anxiety, addiction, fear of intimacy, sexual dysfunction, and a host of other concerns are likely related to unresolved feelings of loss, *even if the client denies any connection is possible*. Whatever the presenting problem or problems may be, it's essential that you be on the lookout for repressed emotions related to losses he may have experienced as a youngster or as an adult.

In my own work as a therapist I see that negative childhood experiences affect the lives of most of my clients in one form or another. When ignored they can trigger self-destructive patterns that may be perpetuated in adulthood, and in my clients' efforts to cope. Even when the presenting problem involves a loss experienced in adulthood, inevitably I find the more recent event has triggered an unresolved loss that occurred at an early age.

Martha was a thirty-eight-year-old website designer who was struggling to sustain her relationship with Tony, a man she'd been seeing for nearly two years. She cared deeply for him, and he had been pressing her to move the relationship to the next step—he wanted to become engaged. But recently they'd begun doing an emotional push-and-pull dance that left them both frustrated and angry. On one hand Martha felt needy and neglected. She wanted Tony to spend more time at her apartment, sharing routine housekeeping chores such as grocery shopping and cleaning. He was happy to comply. But when he did, Martha began to feel crowded, and wanted her "independence" back, so she pushed him away. The cycle repeated itself several times, until one weekend Martha exploded in anger. She demanded Tony leave at once and stay away, insisting she needed "room to breathe."

As Martha recounted the events to me, she acknowledged that she wasn't being fair to Tony, and that he was doing his best to meet her ever-changing demands. Still, the feelings of wanting him to be more involved in her life and wanting him to "give her space" were both very real for her. In fact, she admitted that sometimes she felt like pulling him closer and pushing him away all at the same time. The conflict left her feeling frustrated, frightened, confused, and very lonely.

When I asked her to think of another time she had felt frustrated, frightened, confused, and lonely, she became very quiet…and then a deep sadness filled her eyes as she recalled a day she hadn't thought about in many, many years. She told me about a time when she was eight years old, and returned home from school after being bullied by a girl in her class. Frightened and in tears, she went in search of her mother, who was working in her home office just beyond the kitchen. Martha's mother was on the phone, and put her customer on hold just long enough to usher her young daughter out the door with stern instructions not to bother Mommy while she worked.

As I revisited the experience with Martha, she was able to recognize that the event was one of many in which she had not received the nurturing and support she desperately needed. Together we explored the deep sense of loss she'd experienced as a child as a result of her parents' emotional neglect. I encouraged her to spend some time experiencing the emotions the loss triggered in her, and sat quietly with her as she sobbed—undoubtedly the first time those emotions had been allowed to flow freely, witnessed by another.

When Martha's tears subsided, we discussed the ways her parents' emotional neglect had been experienced as a loss by her eight-year-old mind. At that tender age she was just beginning to comprehend the loss of the care and nurturing of the most important people in her life, and of the safety and security she craved. But at that age, and without the support of understanding caregivers, she lacked the ability to process and assimilate the loss and the emotions that came with it. And so, she repressed them.

Thirty years later those emotions were still present in her unconscious mind, and threatened to undermine her relationship with Tony. Without realizing it, she had been trying to get him to provide the care and nurturing she hadn't received from her *parents. When he offered it, she pushed him away in an effort to push away the pain she might feel once again should he not be there at some future time when she really needed him.*

Once Martha reclaimed that early experience of loss of parental care and released the emotions associated with it, their power over her was defused. Those push-pull feelings still come up now and then with Tony, but she's able to recognize them for what they are, remember their true source, and make conscious choices about how much intimacy and independence she wants as an adult. When feelings of fear, frustration, or loneliness arise, she's learning to acknowledge them rather than repress them, and to allow them to flow freely and release them.

The vast majority of difficulties your clients bring to you are to some degree rooted in a past experience of loss. Your job, as you work with each client, is to tap gently on the walls of repression and find the clues that will show you where emotions have been buried, and the events that have caused her more pain than she's dared to feel. In the safe space that you create, the two of you together will revisit those events and allow that pain to emerge. This time, with your guidance, she'll learn the skills to manage her feelings no matter how large or frightening they may seem.

When your client is able to uncover those old wounds and the reactions they trigger, she will begin to heal her powerful psychic pain. As she heals, she will have greater access to her authentic self and her wholeness, so she can reclaim the healthy aspects of herself that got buried along with the pain. Getting in touch with the inner unseen reality—that when left hidden can drive her behavior—

will give her more control over her life. As she becomes more comfortable with who she is, she can reclaim the energy she's been spending avoiding her pain, controlling her anger, or running from her fear. This healing will open the way to greater intimacy in her relationships, and give her strength in her search for purpose and meaning in her life. In the end she'll feel more truly alive and able to build the life she truly desires.

Chapter Three

Unearthing Past Experiences of Loss

It's a rare client who comes to his first appointment asking for help with an experience of loss. Even one who does may be unaware that a much earlier loss, and the unresolved emotions it generated, is the real reason the recent event is so painful. It's up to you to guide each patient through the process of discovering which experiences are impacting him now—even if those experiences occurred many, many years ago—and bringing them into the light of day. But how will you know where to look?

Without a doubt, your greatest insight will arise from your innate awareness and mindfulness. In addition, fearlessly exploring your own life experience with loss will make you far more adept at recognizing it in others.

However, you can amplify your skills by implementing a few basic tools that will help you unearth the unresolved losses and buried emotions that make it difficult for your client to function at his best. In this chapter you'll learn to:

- take a complete history of your client's past and present home and work environment;
- assess any current life issues that suggest he's struggling with unresolved loss;
- be observant, so you'll notice the many signs of resistance and repression, or clues that old, unresolved emotions are beginning to stir.

In the context of the safe and supportive relationship you establish (see Chapter Eight, "Treatment Strategies for Healing Unresolved Loss"), if you apply these tools with skill, compassion, and intuition, your client will provide the keys to unlock the door to the events he most needs to explore.

Take a complete history

One of the first things you'll do when you begin work with a new client is take a complete history, so that you can gain a sense of the family and events that shaped her as a child. It may take more than one visit to get the foundation in place, and chances are you'll add to it throughout the course of your work together. A good rule of thumb, however, is that if the client is at all resistant to your taking a history, or otherwise reluctant provide information, respect her need for privacy and her need to maintain control of the pace at which she reveals information to you. A client's history will always reveal itself as you go along in the work, so there's no reason to press her. Her reluctance itself will give you valuable clues about the level of protection she needs, and her anxiety about her past.

An unwillingness to share information about the past may also indicate an uneasiness about the therapeutic process. Clients are often worried about speaking negatively about their parents and loved ones. However, over time they come to see that therapy doesn't seek to blame, but instead searches for the truth of what has happened to them, and then helps them resolve the pain, conflicts, and complex issues rooted in those relationships.

And so, it's important that you remain attuned to your client's comfort and willingness to share information, and be content to gather a history when and as she's able to offer it. With that in mind, there are essential pieces of information that will be helpful when getting started, and gathering those early on will become part of your standard practice.

Here's what you'll need to learn during your first few meetings—or as soon as your client is comfortable sharing the information with you:

- **Her description of the reason she came to therapy.** You'll need to know what her symptoms are, what emotions are stirring, how long she's been feeling this way. Once you've established a foundation of trust, ask if there was a time earlier in her life when she remembers having similar symptoms or emotions. Her answer may help lead you to the original unresolved loss. Keep in mind that the reason she gives you for seeking counseling now may be a good assessment of the relevant issues, or it may be just the tip of the iceberg. In some cases it may even be a diversion if the core issue is too painful for her to face.

- **Personal data.** It's good to know your client's age as well as her current marital status and whether she's ever been married, engaged, widowed, or divorced.

- **Her current living arrangement.** Is she living alone or with a spouse, roommate, or family member? What is the nature of her relationship with the person or people she lives with?

- **Her work life.** If she has a job, find out if she enjoys her work, if she's underperforming, or if she's a workaholic. If she doesn't work, ask about primary activities, how she spends her days.

- **Her description of her parents or caretakers.** Find out if they are alive, if she was left by them at an early age, how old they are now (that will tell you if they were very young or very old when they were raising your client), their work life (whether they modeled enjoying their work).

- **A description of her relationship with her parents or caretakers when she was a child, and what it's like now.** Of course, the answer you get initially may not be a literal account of the whole truth. Refer to the lists of symptoms in the chapters in Part Two, "Your Client's Experience," to help you watch for signs that there's more to the story.

- **The family constellation.** Learn the basic structure of the family she grew up in. Were both parents present in the home? If there was a divorce, how old was she when it occurred? Learn the number and gender of siblings, along with birth order. Find out whether there were other extended family members, such as grandparents, aunts, uncles, or cousins, who played a significant role.
- **An overview of family dynamics.** Important details will emerge over time, but at the outset try to get a broad sense of how the family interacted, and how it felt to be a member of that family. Was one parent more dominant or passive than the other? What roles did your client and her siblings play in the family script?
- **Her support system.** Is her family supportive? Does she have friends who are?
- **Health and medical history.** If she's had any serious illnesses or injuries find out when, and the circumstances surrounding their onset and healing.
- **Self-destructive or suicidal thoughts or behaviors.** She may not be entirely forthcoming, but it's critical that you do your best to find out if your client is at risk of hurting herself.

While you're in the process of taking the history, be alert for clues that suggest an area that warrants further exploration later on. Any reluctance to discuss a piece of history or a family member can be a sign that there's a memory of pain attached. Watch your client's facial expressions and body language for signs of tension or sadness as you ask a question or as she gives an answer. Notice, too, any inappropriately positive emotions. For example, if she smiles or laughs as she tells you her father had a terrible temper, it may be a sign that she's buried the pain she experienced during his outbursts. You'll want to dig deeper as time goes on, and help her explore how it really felt to be in that environment. (See also "Be Observant" on page 30 in this chapter.)

Assess current life issues

Everything that happens in your client's life is part of a single tapestry that makes her who she is and that tells the story of her life. Her stated reason for coming to see you is like a loose thread waiting to be examined. Tug on it, and you'll begin to unravel the complex network of unresolved issues the two of you will explore together. The presenting difficulty may in fact be the focus of her healing process, and point directly to the most relevant unresolved loss that needs attention. But chances are that other issues will emerge that will also need to be addressed, and may indeed prove to be more significant components of her recovery than she realized. There may even be aberrant behaviors that you spot, but that she has no idea are inconsistent with those of a healthy, fully functioning individual. In all cases, the struggles she faces in her day-to-day life during the time she's in treatment with you will contribute to your understanding of how her past experiences of loss and unresolved emotions impact her choices, behavior, and happiness today.

With that in mind, take notice of everything that's going on in your client's life, and be attuned to things that may be significant, even if she's unaware they they're at all relevant. Listen and watch, and don't take anything for granted. Clients come to therapy because there's something they don't know. It's our job as therapists to help them look beneath the edges of their awareness to reveal the truths they didn't know they were looking for.

Let's look at some examples. If a client comes to you seeking help with her marriage, and happens to mention a problem with her boss, the trouble at work may hold a clue to what's making it difficult for her to be emotionally present with her spouse. Or if a middle-aged man enters therapy because of anxiety issues, and mentions he hasn't been in a relationship in fifteen years, the reasons for his isolation may also be the cause of his anxiety—even if he says he just likes being single.

Here are a few more life circumstances that may point to a deeper issue of unresolved loss and emotion:

- Your client reports an ongoing state of dread, anxiety, or depression.
- A minor event occurs, and she has an emotional response that's out of proportion to the event that triggered it.
- He repeatedly turns down social invitations.
- Your client is an underachiever. That is, she declines a promotion, or is working in a job that is clearly beneath her skill level or intellectual abilities.

Any of these clues and countless others may provide the key that unlocks a treasure trove of psychological material.

Be observant

One of your most valuable skills as an effective therapist is your power of observation. Again and again throughout the course of each session, your client will give you clues that may tell you far more than the words he speaks. The more adept you are at tuning in to his facial expressions, mannerisms, speech patterns, body language, and other behaviors, the better you'll be able to uncover the issues that lie beyond his conscious awareness.

- **Facial expressions.** Your client's true feelings may be etched in his face, even if he's unable to articulate them with words. In fact, research has demonstrated that making facial gestures is an unconscious process, and a valuable indicator of unconscious thoughts and emotions. By watching for subtle clues, you may more quickly gain an understanding of what's going on beneath the surface, as when a man talks about his girlfriend in what appears to be a neutral discussion, but his upper lip is slightly curled. Conversely, a smile that accompanies a gruesome tale of abuse is a good indication that he's working hard to avoid feeling how painful it was—or to spare *you* from knowing how painful it was.

- **Mannerisms.** Does your client cover her mouth when she speaks about her brother? Does she chew on her lip whenever you ask her about visits to her grandmother's house? Watch for signs that she's hiding from you or from the truth, or that she's anxious or fearful, or even biting back words. Any of these can indicate you're getting close to an event that carries unresolved loss and emotion. As you begin to get to know a client, more and more information will emerge through nonverbal clues. For example, I work with a woman who always touches the corner of her eye when she talks about something that makes her uncomfortable, even though she otherwise appears neutral. Another client will start fingering her earrings whenever she begins to get angry, as if she is self-soothing so as not to lose control.

- **Speech patterns.** If his voice suddenly becomes very quiet, or if he begins to mumble, take note. If he's normally very articulate, but has trouble finding the words to describe the way it felt when his wife came home late from work, it may be a sign there's an unresolved emotion that's lurking beneath his effort to casually brush off the incident.

- **Body language.** Learning to read body language is a skill you can acquire with careful attention, and an art you can cultivate with extensive study. Many books are available on the subject, and it's worth your time to explore one or two. Begin by applying your interpersonal skills and intuition, and watch for signs of tension or withdrawal. Nervous tension may be expressed through a tapping foot or shoulders that creep up around the neck. An unconscious desire to withdraw or hide from the subject at hand might cause your client's body to appear to contract, or become concave, with shoulders curling in around the chest. Any of these gestures could mean you've entered territory that requires further exploration.

- **Fluctuations in cognitive states.** Sometimes it seems as though the fog rolls in, and your client can't sustain a train of thought or even remember what he was talking about a few seconds ago. Assuming your client has no intellectual impairment, this could be a signal that he is in internal conflict. In other words, as he is talking, either new memories or new affect begin to interfere with what he is accustomed to thinking or saying about a topic. This is why it is unavoidable—and valuable—that a client tell you the same story again and again, because with each retelling something new will emerge, even if it is not very obvious to him.

  In other cases he may nimbly skip from one subject to another, oblivious to the fact that he's made the switch mid-sentence. This might indicate he's getting too close to a new idea or awareness, and his mind is literally struggling to hold on to the old defense while something new is emerging. It's also possible his unconscious mind is blithely rerouting him away from a subject that seems too painful to explore.

  Events like these, or similar fluctuations in cognitive state, can be signs you're venturing into an area your client has worked hard to repress.

✦ ✦ ✦

As you apply these tools throughout the course of your work together you'll unearth the losses and buried emotions that are at the root of the difficulties your client faces today. When those losses reveal themselves to you, you'll be better prepared to recognize them as such. We know that loss can take many, many forms, and in the coming chapters we'll explore the vast range of circumstances your client may have experienced in this way. When you're able to recognize those circumstances for what they are, you'll be ready to be a catalyst for the healing your client needs.

It is not our job as therapists to provide answers, but rather to find the essential questions and instill curiosity in our clients. If we do that job well, we will guide them to discover the truth about their lives, so they can put feelings to their thoughts and experiences and get in touch with their deepest needs and desires.

PART TWO

Your Client's Experience

CHAPTER FOUR

When Safety, Self-Worth, and Boundaries Are Violated

Physical & Sexual Abuse, Emotional Abuse & Neglect, Domestic Violence

In an ideal world, the home and family provide a safe and comforting environment where a child can develop a core sense of safety that will sustain him throughout his life. But too often physical, sexual, or emotional abuse shatters that sense of safety and disrupts the development of a healthy sense of self-worth. Even when the child is not the target, violence between other family members makes the world seem a frightening, uncertain place. In any of these circumstances a child loses those essential feelings of safety and self-worth. Until the loss is addressed, his ability to function will be compromised into adulthood.

Many of the clients who enter your office are there because of unresolved issues of loss just like these, from events that occurred when they were very young. As a result they may face a range of difficulties due to a compromised sense of self. They may even be in an abusive relationship as an adult (and may not even realize it). Your ability to help them understand how and when those first losses occurred will enable them to take the first steps toward resolution and healing.

Physical and Sexual Abuse

Any treatment that is not in the best interest of the victim constitutes abuse. Physical abuse, such as punching, slapping, spanking, pushing, pulling, kicking, shaking, pinching, or burning, is often the easiest to identify because of visible evidence. It may leave bruises, cuts, burns, scars, or other marks, and cause pain, broken bones, or internal injuries—or it might not. In any case, after the physical body heals from abuse, the emotional scars remain. The victim must find a way to live with the terror and pain of such mistreatment. Children are vulnerable to believing they caused the abuse, leading to feelings of guilt, shame, and helplessness. These feelings can remain into adulthood, and have a devastating impact on mental health.

Sexual abuse is any sexual conduct between an adult and a child or between an older child and a younger child. *Any* form of sexual contact of this kind is inappropriate and harmful, whether it is covert or overt, ranging from flirtation to fondling to sexual intercourse to showing the child pornography. Even talking to a child about sex or sexual acts—outside of age-appropriate education by a responsible adult—is experienced by the child as abuse.

Boys as well as girls can be victims of sexual abuse. And anyone can be an abuser, especially if he or she is perceived by the child as an authority figure. That may include a parent, brother, sister, uncle, aunt, friend, teacher, neighbor, doctor, priest—the list is endless.

Emotional Abuse and Neglect

An unhealthy relationship can be shattering to an individual's well-being even in the complete absence of physical contact. Any behavior that is designed to control and subordinate another human being through the use of fear, intimidation, humiliation, guilt, coercion, or manipulation constitutes abuse. Yelling and threatening, making quiet derogatory comments, or withholding love and support can make an individual feel unloved, unwanted, unsafe, or worthless. Under the guise of "helpful guidance" abusers may offer criticism or sarcasm, hold their victims to unrealistic expectations, or compare them negatively to their peers. In other cases a child may be expected to fulfill an emotional void in the parent, so that his ability to develop a healthy autonomy is compromised.

Such behavior may not leave physical bruises or scars, but the damage is just as real. Eventually the victim loses all sense of self, along with any remnant of belief in his personal value. With emotional abuse, the insults, insinuations, criticism, and accusations slowly eat away at his self-esteem until he is incapable of judging the situation realistically, and often blames himself for the abuse. To be neglected as a child means, in essence, psychically, not to exist. His very presence in the world goes unnoticed, and he's left feeling empty and invisible, with a core belief that his needs are unimportant and his presence in the world irrelevant.

One of the challenges of dealing with emotional abuse or neglect is that, unlike physical abuse, it may be difficult to recognize or identify. Consequently the impact can be more insidious, as the victim may be unaware he has been abused. The perpetrator, when confronted, may readily acknowledge her behavior but not recognize it as abusive, especially when the behavior was modeled by her own parents and grandparents, as is often the case.

Domestic Violence

Domestic violence can be defined as physical or emotional abuse that occurs between two adults. A child who grows up under the shadow of domestic violence is as much a victim as the adult at whom the blows or insults are aimed. As with other forms of abuse, the perpetrator uses fear, guilt, shame, intimidation, physical violence, or threats of harm—to the victim or other family members—to gain power, domination, and control. He may also withhold money, credit cards, or basic necessities such as food, clothes, or medications, or prevent the victim from working, so that she remains dependent upon her abuser. The victim may feel responsible for provoking the attacks and, with eroded self-esteem, powerless to resist or to end the relationship.

A child living with violence in the family internalizes many of the losses of the abused adult, along with guilt and powerlessness for his inability to protect her. Because his parents are incapable of creating nurturing bonds with their child, he is at significant risk of suffering abuse or neglect. He also suffers the loss of an opportunity to witness a healthy adult relationship, and instead absorbs the negative modeling of the violent relationship. He faces a high risk of engaging in violent relationships as an adult—as an abuser or a victim.

What Is Lost

A child who experiences physical, sexual, or emotional abuse or neglect loses her sense of value as a human being. The message delivered with every blow or every derogatory comment is, "You don't matter." When trusted individuals administer treatment that feels terrible, the child loses the ability to trust her own perceptions and emotions. As her physical and emotional space is violated, she loses the ability to establish healthy boundaries between herself and others. With her needs and wants unheard and ignored, her sense of personal power is lost. And when the parents she loves treat her and one another with cruelty or violence, she loses the core belief that she deserves to be treated with tenderness and respect, and begins to see negative treatment as the norm. Ultimately she loses her innate sense of safety, and experiences the world as a place where fear and suffering are inevitable.

It's impossible to identify every loss that may occur as a result of exposure to abuse and violence. Every individual—every client—responds differently. But the following list will serve as a brief reference to guide you as you investigate what *your* client may have lost as a result of his unique experience:

- A sense of personal value, self worth, or self esteem
- A sense of trust and safety in relationships, and in the world at large
- The experience of having his physical and emotional boundaries identified and respected
- Personal power
- Modeling and support for being present with emotions and expressing them in a healthy way
- The experience of being loved and cherished
- An opportunity to witness support and care between people
- Modeling in what a respectful, loving relationship looks and feels like
- An opportunity to learn to identify his needs and ask—and expect—that they be met
- The joyful, secure childhood that everyone is entitled to

The Long-Term Impact

Lana came into therapy because her husband's verbal abuse had escalated, and he'd begun to push and slap her. He often demanded to have sex with her on command, and if she didn't want sex he would "make her." They'd been married three years, and she wanted to explore what she was doing to cause his aggressive behavior, and how she could avoid provoking him.

When we discussed the early days of her relationship with her husband, she began to realize that although he was charismatic and romantic, she had actually noticed early signs that he was controlling and aggressive. She'd overlooked them, though, thinking that "it wasn't such a big deal." She continued to rationalize that he'd had a hard childhood and that he didn't mean to behave badly. When I asked her to consider that forcing her to have sex was essentially rape, she was shocked, and steadfast in her denial.

Over the course of several months of work, Lana began to realize that her husband reminded her of her father, who could also be charismatic but who used to endlessly criticize and ridicule her mother. He also liked to have Lana play a game of "sitting on his lap," during which he would touch her genitals and make her do the same to him. Although this memory was painful to revisit, discussing it began to free her from the secret of abuse she had carried for thirty years. In time she came to see the similarities between her father's behavior and that of her husband. As she began to regain the sense of self-worth she had lost as a result of her father's abuse, she reclaimed her voice, practiced setting healthy boundaries, and redefined how she wanted to be treated in her relationship. Ultimately she was able to leave her marriage.

Imagine what would happen if a strong woman with a healthy sense of her personal value encountered a man like the one Lana had found when she first met her husband. At the first sign of abusive or controlling behavior, she'd let him know she expected to be treated with respect and consideration. When he didn't clean up his act she'd walk away, well aware that she deserved better, and unwilling to settle for less.

But when Lana met that same man she found someone who treated her the way she expected to be treated, the way she felt she deserved to be treated. Like so many victims of abuse and domestic violence she was drawn to what was familiar—after all, he "felt like family" from the start. And her poor sense of self-worth allowed her to believe the abusive behavior was okay. Until she came into therapy it never occurred to her that she had the power to say no—to the verbal abuse, the slapping, or the rape. Lana's relationship with her husband was a direct outgrowth of the unresolved losses she experienced as a child.

Lana's situation is not unique. Individuals who grew up with abuse and violence are extremely likely to enter abusive relationships themselves—and stay in them—because:

- it's familiar, what's been modeled for them;
- their loss of a sense of self-worth lets them believe it's what they deserve;
- their loss of personal power makes them feel unable to resist or walk away;
- they become so convinced they are worthless that they believe no one else could want them, and therefore they have nowhere else to go;
- their ultimate fear is being all alone.

But survivors of abuse don't always assume the role of victim. In many cases they become abusers themselves, reenacting the destructive behavior that was once directed at them or another family member. Like Lana they, too, are expressing behavior that was modeled for them. However, their loss of power as a child drives them to desperately seek power and control over others, and they strive to elevate their poor sense of self-worth by demeaning and manipulating others. While not every victim of abuse becomes an abuser—far from it—it is safe to say that virtually every abuser was a victim at some time.

It's not uncommon for the child of an abusive family to become an abuser in some relationships and a recipient of abuse in others. For example, they may tend to be abused in romantic relationships, allowing their partners to define and control them. In friendships, however, they may play the role of abuser by withholding attention or approval, offering "helpful" criticism, manipulating, making excessive demands, becoming enmeshed or co-dependent, and so forth. Victims may avoid parenting altogether, try to be the perfect parent, or—the worst possible consequence—perpetuate the abuse onto the next generation. In all cases, their behavior is likely to be similar to the behavior they observed in the abusive family member or learned in their efforts to survive.

What's clear is that the losses incurred during a childhood steeped in abuse very likely, if left unresolved, lead to ongoing struggles in relationships. Indeed, they scar virtually all facets of the victim's life, since she or he is left with little or no self-esteem. Many emotional problems can emerge from the abuse, including an inability to trust, phobias, avoidance of intimacy, depression, anxiety, anger, hostility, defiance, antisocial tendencies, even criminal behavior. When a parent held excessively high standards for the child or a spouse as a prerequisite for winning approval, attention, and love, the child may grow into an adult driven by perfectionism. While perfectionism itself can be crippling, it also often leads individuals to feelings of insecurity, vulnerability, shame, and hopelessness. A survivor may have trouble coping with the routine challenges of life, and become overwhelmed with negativity and gloom as a result. Emotional detachment is also common, with isolation and a failure to learn to develop sympathy, empathy, and other important relational attributes. This can result in difficulty socializing and an inability to develop meaningful friendships.

Adults who were raised in homes with domestic violence have been shown to experience more anxiety than children who were not exposed. They grew up in continual fear of the next violent act, towards them or others in the family, and the fear that one or both parents would abandon them. As a result, their latent anxiety can develop into panic disorder, phobias, and other maladaptive defenses.

Survivors of sexual abuse often have problems developing a healthy sexuality. Some may confuse sex with love. One client of mine captured this very succinctly when she said, "The only time my father gave me any attention was in bed. I was special to him then. I felt loved." Like her, these individuals may seek casual sexual encounters in an effort to satisfy their longing for tenderness. They may become promiscuous, and are vulnerable to finding partners who are uninterested in a meaningful relationship, leaving the victim feeling further victimized. The opposite can be true if the sexual abuse was violent. These individuals may confuse sex with domination and power, and fear being controlled and manipulated while having sex. As a result, they may be unwilling to risk any physical intimacy, or do so only with great trepidation.

A common thread among victims of physical and sexual abuse, emotional abuse and neglect, and domestic violence is difficulty accessing and expressing emotions. Denial and repression of the fear and heartache were valuable coping mechanisms when living helplessly in the midst of a terrible situation. But reclaiming those emotions does not come easily, and the patterns of denial often remain into adulthood—as does the buried pain. Without the ability to express their pain directly, with words, victims may resort to self-destructive behavior as a covert way of expressing suffering, and as a reaction to their childhood experience of not having control over their bodies. Alcoholism, drug abuse, emotional eating, anorexia or bulimia, sleep disorders, and cutting are some of the ways victims express their pain while exerting some form of control over the bodies that their abusers once unjustly claimed. Some resort to suicide when the unexpressed pain and rage become too much to bear.

Sadly, while abuse and violence in the home are tragically prevalent in our society, a relative few victims ever seek treatment. In many segments of our culture there remains a substantial stigma attached to these behaviors, and coming forward to acknowledge and address the issues in one's own family is rife with guilt and shame—particularly for a victim with a well-developed tendency to feel guilt and shame. What's more, the need for the child—and the child within the adult—to see his parents as protectors, and to accept blame for his troubles so he can hold on to the belief that they really did love and care for him, makes it particularly difficult for him to gain the clarity necessary to name his abuse and his abusers. This cloud does have a silver lining, though, in that many survivors find themselves with less threatening reasons to seek therapy. In the comfort and safety of your office, and under your skilled and gentle guidance, they will, when they're ready, begin to look for the deeper causes of their struggles.

Presenting Symptoms

Some of the clients who are dealing with the types of loss we've considered in this chapter will be aware that their history of abuse is at least part of the problem, and lay those cards on the table when they arrive in your office. However, many will seek help because of seemingly (to them) unrelated issues in their present-day lives, such as difficulty in relationships, sleep disorders, anxiety, or depression. These clients are either:

- aware there was trouble in their childhood home but completely unaware of any connection to their current difficulties;

- aware of the connection but ashamed or fearful about discussing it; or

- genuinely unaware that they were abused, because they're deep in denial or still steeped in the practice of defending their abusers.

Often it will be up to you, then, to discern whether a history of abuse or violence plays a role in the issues your clients bring to your sessions. Valuable information will be available to you as you take a careful history (see Chapter Eight, "Treatment Strategies Based on an Understanding of Loss"). However, keep in mind that one of the hallmarks of abuse is the victim's need to protect and defend her abuser. In fact, reporting an idyllic childhood may itself be an indication that some degree of denial is in play. If your client insists she had an unwaveringly loving and supportive family, retain a healthy bit of skepticism until you've confirmed beyond any reasonable doubt that that's the case. I sometimes wonder if anyone has escaped the pain of some form of emotional abuse or neglect. Be sure to keep your eyes, ears, and intuition alert for any indication your client is one of the many who carry this burden.

Fortunately, your clients have many ways of letting you know the real story, even when it's too difficult for them to put it into words. The long-term impact of abuse, and the symptoms of that impact, will provide you with plenty of clues to point you in the right direction. For example, as we know, victims of childhood abuse often engage in abusive relationships as adults. But like their parents they may be in utter denial that there's anything unhealthy about their current relationships. Obvious signs of aggressive or threatening behavior will be a clear indication that there's trouble. But often the clues are more subtle. Look for symptoms of problematic relationships in the way they interact with you, and in the stories they tell you about interactions with partners, family members, friends, or others. If they're reenacting the destructive modeling they experienced as a child—now playing the role of victim, abuser, or both—they may:

- deliberately start arguments;
- be in continuous conflict with others;
- casually mention that a partner has a bad or short temper;
- indicate a need to ask a partner's permission before making a decision or planning an activity;
- invalidate others' reality, as in, "I didn't say that," "That's not what I meant," or "You're too sensitive";
- suppress or ignore their feelings, or be unwilling to express them;
- play on others' fear, guilt, or compassion to get what they want;
- attempt to gain control by threatening to end a relationship;
- withdraw attention or affection, using "silent treatment" or "a cold shoulder" to control or manipulate;
- lack clearly defined personal limits and boundaries, and so become enmeshed in partners', friends', and family members' needs and emotions;

- be unpredictable and inconsistent, saying one thing one day and something else the next (and then denying doing it);
- be continually hyper-vigilant, always on guard for the next change of mood, outburst, or unpredictable behavior;
- passively accept abusive behavior;
- accept responsibility for a partner's abusive behavior;
- report that they must "walk on egg shells" at home;
- feel consistently frightened, unsettled, anxious, or off balance;
- have difficulty with intimacy, security, trust, and commitment.

Beyond the scope of close personal relationships, the diminished sense of self-worth, personal power, healthy boundaries, and other losses that result from abuse and violence during childhood express themselves in a predictable pattern of symptoms that affect every aspect of the victim's life. The following list will help you develop a broader picture of the habits and behaviors that suggest this is an area you'll need to explore:

- A reluctance to stand up for herself or act in her own best interest, or feelings of guilt when she does
- A tendency to defer to others' needs and opinions at the expense of her own

- Denying, minimizing, or repressing her feelings
- Difficulty with intimacy and commitment
- Pervasive negativity regarding herself, her life, and the world in general
- Isolation
- Emotional detachment
- A quickness to anger; difficulty with anger management
- Excessive passivity, anxiety, submission, or aggression around authority figures
- An unreasonable willingness to tolerate abuse, endure pain, or remain submissive in a difficult circumstance
- Addictive behaviors, including alcoholism, drug abuse, emotional eating, or excessive gambling (see Chapter Six, "When Physical and Emotional Health Is Disrupted")
- Bulimia or anorexia
- Obesity or emaciation
- Identifying sex with love; promiscuity
- Identifying sex with control and aggression; aversion to sex
- Chronic or recurring physical ailments, such as migraines, back and stomach pains, fatigue, or insomnia
- Perfectionism
- Hopelessness

- Helplessness
- Inappropriate shame or guilt
- Fear of abandonment
- Fear of criticism
- Fear of failure
- An aversion to taking risks
- Anxiety or panic disorder
- Phobias
- Poor social skills, or a reported history of poor skills as a child
- A history of poor school performance
- Anger, hostility, defiance, antisocial tendencies, or criminal behavior
- Suicidal thoughts

✦ ✦ ✦

Admittedly, when one's sense of safety, self-worth, and boundaries are violated as they are when a child experiences abuse, neglect, or violence, the scope of the loss is profound, and the long-term impact can seem dismal. But by making her first appointment your client has already taken a vital step toward the healing that will resolve the emotional impact of that loss. Often, a victim of abuse will need to go through a great deal of pain before she tires of the consequences, and it is then that she becomes willing to work on core issues and begin living her life as a survivor rather than a victim. Changing the self-destructive patterns of behavior and recovering from childhood abuse is a slow process, but one that can in fact yield a successful, rewarding outcome. With your client's strength and courage and your skill, compassion, and dedication, the two of you will find the peace and healing she so richly deserves.

CHAPTER FIVE

When the Family Unit Is Broken

Divorce and Adoption

As we have seen, family is meant to be a source of safety, comfort, and security, an environment in which a child can develop an innate sense that he is of value, that the world is a safe place, and that the people he loves are people he can trust. But when divorce or adoption tears that family unit apart, the child feels abandoned by the very people on whom he depends for his safety, comfort, and security.

Deep human insecurities surround abandonment. It is one of the most basic of all our fears, perhaps second only to death. On an emotional level it triggers the dread of being left alone and uncared for. The grief of abandonment is a profound form of bereavement, complicated by the sense of rejection and betrayal. The core feelings of safety and security are damaged, and the child's sense of self-worth and his ability to trust may be lost.

To make matters worse, we live in a society that is reluctant to talk about "personal family matters" or the messy emotions that go along with them. As a result, the many people touched by a divorce or an adoption must endure their pain and grief and fears in silence. Inevitably the emotions become buried under layers of denial and repression, so that the initial losses are compounded as their impact is extended for years, into every corner of life.

As you examine the various ways these losses may impact your clients, you'll gain the understanding you need to help them reclaim their sense of self-worth and their trust in the world.

Divorce

Divorce is by far one of the most painful and discombobulating losses your client can experience. It's the death of a dream, of the vision of living with a partner as a family unit "till death do us part." When that family falls apart, along with the emotional pain there is often financial hardship, the loss of home and belongings, perhaps even the loss of friendships and extended family members. A similar traumatic loss may also occur with the end of a romantic relationship or long-term friendship. However, divorce carries the added burden of the disruption of the socially sanctioned family unit, and the potential for stigma and the guilt or shame that go with it.

The child of a divorce also suffers deeply. He struggles to understand what it means for parents to want to live apart, and often assumes he caused the split. When the family structure dissolves, his sense of security dissolves along with it, and fear, anxiety, and anger are likely to take its place. He may be required to sleep in two different bedrooms in two separate homes. Not only is his home life disrupted, but he may also face a change of schools and a loss of friendships. And while a divorcing adult can hope to one day find a new spouse, a child can never hope to find new parents.

Adoption

There are more than four million adopted children in America today, and another 300,000 children cycle through foster care each and every year. Millions more are affected—adult adoptees, their partners, children, and friends, the birth mothers and their families, and the adoptive families.

When a child is separated from his mother, no matter how justifiable and necessary it is, no matter how attentive and conscientious his caregivers are, he experiences the separation as abandonment. For a child of any age, abandonment is an unthinkable loss. Although adoption provides a solution, the experience can come with its own set of problems. We tend to regard it as a seamless happy ending with no long-term effect on the child, the adoptive parents, or the birth mother. But the experience of loss for all parties is profound and lasting, particularly in a society that is conflicted about the issue of childhood abandonment, with a widespread reluctance to openly address the problem. The idealized view of adoption that has evolved as a result is at the heart of the dilemma.

The adoption triad

When we consider who has the potential to suffer as a result of adoption, we're quick to think of the adopted child marked by early abandonment and facing the need to reconcile a relationship with two sets of parents. Our thoughts may then turn to the birth mother forced to make the heart-tearing decision to give up her child. But we often don't realize the adoptive parents may also suffer in silence, and need the support and healing that therapy can provide. In your work with any member of the adoption triad, be prepared to acknowledge the losses that *all* parties may have endured.

- **The child's abandonment.** The plight of the adopted child is heart wrenching by any standard. In addition to grief, fear, and isolation, she experiences a deep sense of shame at being given away. Often adopted children are not told of their origins. Some are told as teenagers. Others are never told, and learn of their first family only on the death of their adoptive parents. When the adoptive family is silent about the adoption, it's perceived by the child as further evidence of the shame of her circumstances. As a result, many adopted children feel they must not speak of their abandonment, and they mourn in silence. The community and the family ensure this silence with well-meaning comments such as, "You were lucky to be adopted," "Your parents really love you," or, "I grew up wishing I was adopted." Cast adrift, the child may find herself navigating life feeling alone, afraid, confused, and grief stricken.

How can we talk about infant and childhood mourning when we can't bear the thought of its existence? How can an infant or a child mourn the loss of a parent they may never have known? We seem to think that if we don't talk about these problems, maybe they don't exist. This leaves the adopted child and her new family silenced. It also prevents parents from being in touch with their child's pain. Yet how can a child possibly talk about such a loss without the support and guidance of her adoptive parents? The simple answer is that she can't and she doesn't.

- **The birth mother's dilemma.** To lose a child is a devastating heartbreak for any woman. As if that weren't enough, the birth mother must also deal with the stigma of having given up her child. It's an issue that crosses social, moral, and religious codes, and may also have legal implications. A majority of women who give up their children are unmarried, and while the stigma of having a child out of wedlock has decreased dramatically in recent years, in some families and cultures it remains a source of shame. Without a doubt, for a woman who gave up her child ten or twenty or more years ago, the taboo against unmarried pregnancy was so enormous that it marked her life forever.

  As a result, the birth mother may have a profound sense of shame. Of course, there's also the grief of being separated from her child, and in knowing that she cannot provide for her baby or be there to love and nurture her. The mother also may be angry—angry at herself for being in the circumstances that led her to give up her child, angry that the birth father and her own family did not provide the support that would have enabled her to keep her baby, and angry at society and the system that forced her to abandon her child. The woman who places her child for adoption often spends her whole life in mourning, because it's unlikely she'll have an opportunity to talk about it, let alone grieve openly. Her shame may be so great that there is no room for grief. She might also feel the judgment of those around her in spoken or implied messages, such as, "You made the decision, you wanted to give the kid up, so you have no right to complain." As a result, there is no release for her sorrow and grief.

- **The adoptive parents' grief.** Adoptive parents are usually an infertile couple who want children, but who are unable to conceive or plagued by a series of miscarriages. Therefore, the adoptive family is born out of grief and loss. There is also shame at not being able to conceive naturally or to give birth to one's own children. In many traditional cultures, infertility brands a woman as a second-class citizen. In their disappointment, the infertile couple may try to hide their emotions from themselves, from one another, and from family and friends. Their grief is rarely acknowledged or mourned openly. But unless or until they go through a mourning process to resolve their loss, they will never be able to fully open their hearts to love their new child.

For the new parents, the very presence of their adopted child may be a painful reminder of their unresolved loss, the inability to carry their own healthy child to term. If the child is strikingly different from the family in physical appearance or personality, that is another constant reminder of the absence of a biological connection.

There are so many conflicts and unmet needs in this situation—the yearning of the parents to see themselves and their identity reflected in their children, the need for the child to find himself in another and to receive love in return, the shame that prevents anyone from freely acknowledging their pain. In this maze of emotions, the adoptive parents may also feel unconscious anger at the birth mother for conceiving when they could not. Eventually the adoptive family—parents as well as the child—may just give up on each other because of unspoken grief.

What Is Lost

Anyone whose life is touched by divorce or adoption must endure the loss of the stability of the family unit, and the shattered dreams and expectations for what his life would be like within that family. Ultimately the experience leads to a loss of the core sense of safety and trust—both critical to the formation of a healthy belief in one's value in the world. Along with profound feelings of abandonment, divorce often leaves its survivors feeling unworthy of the love they so desperately want and need. The child given up at birth has lost the opportunity to experience the safety and security that foster a core sense of self-worth at a critical moment in his development. He loses a core sense of belonging: "My own mother gave me away. I don't belong anywhere. Who can I trust?" For the birth mother, the terrible choice she must make will inevitably force her to question her self-worth for years to come. The infertility of many adoptive parents also gnaws at their sense of self-worth.

And so, a similar thread runs through the losses experienced by the children of divorce, by adults whose marriage ends in divorce, and by all members of the adoption triad, creating a tapestry of deficits for everyone concerned. The following list will help you be on the lookout for those losses that most deeply impact your client:

- A basic sense of self-worth
- A core sense of security
- The sense of safety and comfort that comes from believing the world is a predictable and reliable place
- A sense of security in knowing someone will always be there to look after her
- The knowledge that she is loved and lovable
- The sense that she is safe and protected
- The ability to trust herself—to make good choices and be important to others
- An ability to trust others—that they will be there tomorrow, keep their promises, and not abandon her
- The belief that she matters, that she is of value in the world

There are some losses that are unique to the dissolution of a marriage or partnership, because a family that was once intact becomes broken. For a divorcing adult as well as a child of divorcing parents, suddenly the world he thought he could count on no longer exists, and the person or people he thought would always be there for him are gone. Every expectation for the future is altered, if not shattered. He may lose his home, his lifestyle, and possibly his larger social network. The list of losses for the child or adult survivor of divorce includes the following:

- The daily presence of two parents who would always be there to love and protect him—or so he thought
- The comfort of a routine, with one house and home and family to come home to every night
- The dream of "happily ever after" with a loving and loved partner
- The love he thought he could count on forever
- The security of the ongoing presence of a partner he's lived with intimately and come to rely on
- His place in his social network
- The support of an extended family of in-laws
- The vision of family and future that was once central to his life
- Financial security and stability
- His house and home

Adoption also carries a unique set of losses. In addition to those listed above, if your client was an adopted child, these losses are likely part of her experience:

- The security of having grown up feeling wanted
- A knowledge of her birth tribe and ancestry
- The ability to feel safe, that abandonment will not strike at any time
- A sense of belonging

Both she and her new mother will have lost the opportunity to achieve the hormonal bonding that occurs naturally between mother and infant during the first hours and days after birth. Adoptive parents and the birth mother are all grieving the loss of the opportunity to raise their own biological child.

The Long-Term Impact

Jon and Emily were both thirty-two when they came to see me for couples therapy. Jon was a respiratory therapist in a local hospital, and Emily was a pediatric nurse in the intensive care unit at the same hospital. They both enjoyed their work and found it rewarding. They had been dating for two years, but felt unable to move forward with their relationship.

Jon reported that he had been living alone since he and his first wife, Mary, had divorced about four years earlier. Emily had a roommate and had never been married. She felt she needed to take their relationship to the next level and wanted to move in together. Jon felt he was "not ready to make that commitment," which made Emily afraid he would never commit. She had urged him to go to couples therapy with her in an effort to sort things out.

Jon's relationship with Mary had ended abruptly after four years of dating and two years of marriage. He had never quite understood why she had ended it—he'd thought they "had it all." He acknowledged he was devastated when the marriage ended, and didn't start dating until two years later. Although he thought he had been grieving during that time, as we explored his experience he realized that he had not actually grieved, but instead had "pulled himself away" from everyone he loved, including his brother, with whom he had always had a close relationship and in whom he'd confided over the years.

Over the course of several months of therapy it became evident that Jon was afraid to make a commitment to Emily for fear she, too, would leave him. After some difficult work he was able to open up more deeply with Emily about his fears, and the feelings of betrayal and sadness he had experienced at the end of his marriage. They were able to work through those unresolved feelings and concerns and eventually established a more intimate and open relationship, which culminated in their moving in together.

Unfortunately Jon's story, with his years of suffering in silence, is much too common. We live in a society that suffers from massive denial about most emotional difficulties. Where divorce and adoption are concerned, with their messy complications around relationships, conflict, and heart-wrenching ethical choices, friends and family are often particularly uncomfortable providing the support that's so desperately needed. Few are willing to provide an understanding ear for the months or years it takes to recover when someone's marriage has fallen apart. They'd much rather see everyone "get over it" and move on. The impact of divorce on children is often wildly underestimated, and divorcing parents may be too distraught to provide the support their youngsters so desperately need. And since adoption is commonly viewed as everyone's happy ending, there's little opportunity for adopted children, their birth mothers, or their adoptive parents to share their heartache. When the emotional consequences that come with any of these losses remain unaddressed, the impact can resonate for years.

The social pressure to suffer in silence is often internalized, so that denial and repression take the place of honest expression of emotions. I see a pattern among adults who come to therapy and describe their childhood memories of their parents' divorce. It usually goes something like this: "Well...they fought all the time and it was horrible. They never spoke to each other and it was so stressful. I was relieved when they separated. They were so much happier after they divorced." I think you get the picture. I hear lots of good examples of rationalization, with clients thinking intellectually about the divorce while suppressing the suffering they experienced.

The grief and fear and anxiety and anger that come with such a dramatic upheaval in a child's basic safety unit are just too much for a youngster to handle. And if his parents weren't talking with him about it, how could the child know how to manage it all? He manages by repressing it, and by finding a piece of the story that makes it all okay. "They were so much happier afterward" may be true enough in the grand scheme of things, but it belies the suffering the child experienced at the time.

Until that suffering is allowed to surface, the feelings of abandonment and the lost ability to trust may impair the child's ability to enter a committed relationship years later. He may continue into adulthood feeling depressed, lonely, sad, and angry. He might feel unsafe emotionally, unable to trust his own instincts, and insecure when making decisions for himself. While the child's performance in school may have suffered when his parents divorced, as an adult he may continue to underperform at work, or perhaps not even pursue work he enjoys or that will be satisfying to him. Addictive behaviors may emerge as he attempts to avoid the old hurts simmering away inside, and the new ones instigated by his ongoing struggles.

When an adult experiences the loss of a divorce, the impact may be just as far-reaching. If his parents' marriage ended when he was a child, his own divorce may trigger unresolved and buried emotions from that early trauma. The sense of abandonment is often profound. He fears that other people he loves will also abandon him, and that he himself may be unlovable. In any case, his core sense of security may be shaken by the collapse of his relationship, and, like Jon, his ability to enter freely and openly into a new committed relationship may be compromised. If he does not allow himself to grieve his loss deeply and freely, depression, anxiety, and addictive behaviors may follow.

Similarly, abandonment and the resulting lost ability to trust often has a lasting impact on the child given up for adoption. Long into adulthood she may fear she will be abandoned yet again. All children—even those living with their biological parents—experience abandonment issues. But for the adopted child these fears are more deeply rooted because she has actually experienced permanent separation from her birth parents. The consequences of this abandonment are reflected in feelings of inferiority or of being defective, unlovable, or invisible. She may have an ongoing sense of not belonging, and difficulty trusting anyone who wants to form a relationship with her.

Much like the child of divorce, her fears can make it difficult to form a healthy and lasting relationship with a significant other. She may choose partners who are emotionally unavailable, or attract others who will eventually abandon her. In her attempt to avoid rejection she might bounce from relationship to relationship. Alternatively, her fear of being alone may lead her to form relationships with anyone to fill the void, or to be unwilling to let go of relationships or situations that are no longer good for her.

For the woman who has given up her child for adoption, her struggle with guilt and shame can make it difficult for her to form meaningful relationships as well. In her belief that she is unworthy or unlovable she may choose partners who treat her as though she has little value, and accept abusive treatment as her due. Even with a loving partner she may remain distant or withdrawn. If she has other children who remain with her, her relationship with them may be remote, as she feels unworthy of their love, appreciation, and respect. If her guilt is not resolved depression, anxiety, and addictive behaviors may develop.

When adoptive parents are unable to resolve their grief over their inability to have biological children of their own, they may have difficulty creating a close and loving relationship with their adopted child. Their shame may cause them to feel undeserving of her affection, and their unspoken longing for a biological child of their own may cause them to become resentful or overly critical of the child. In their desire to avoid facing feelings they believe are inappropriate they may turn to addictive behaviors to mask or bury their pain.

The dual loss of the sense of self-worth and ability to trust are recurring themes for those whose core family unit has been altered by divorce or adoption. The impact will be ongoing until the losses are identified and grieved, the attending emotions acknowledged and released, and the sense of self-worth and ability to trust restored.

Presenting Symptoms

Often, the damaged sense of safety and trust, the feelings of abandonment, and the lost sense of self-worth lie hidden behind a well-established layer of denial. Many people come into therapy unable to understand why they are feeling out of balance; they may know something is wrong without knowing what it is. They may readily report their experience with divorce or adoption, but be unaware of its profound ongoing impact on their emotions and on their lives. It's up to you to help them discover the central issues of loss that prevent them from putting those losses behind them and experiencing the joy and fulfillment they deserve.

The following symptoms are some of the ways these core issues of loss may express themselves in your client. She may:

- avoid talking about her divorce or adoption, or her feelings about it;
- deny the severity of the loss or its impact;
- show signs of isolation, regression, or needy behavior;
- perform poorly at work, or work at a job that is not satisfying or does not utilize her skills or experience;
- have difficulty making decisions;
- express or show evidence of a fear of commitment or of starting a new relationship;
- have difficulty letting go of relationships or situations that are unhealthy;
- indicate an excessive fear of abandonment or betrayal;
- assume an inordinate amount of blame for the end of a relationship;
- excessively blame the other for the end of a relationship;
- show signs of loneliness, anger, depression, or anxiety;
- report or show evidence of using drugs or alcohol, or of other addictive behaviors.

✦ ✦ ✦

Now that your client has come to you for help, she can begin the process of grieving her loss, be it the divorce of her parents or the dissolution of her own marriage, or the many losses that accompany adoption. Once she allows herself to enter the grieving process and ultimately resolves that grief, she can rebuild her lost self-esteem and release her fears about being unworthy. As the healing unfolds she will feel more fully alive and her symptoms will begin to dissipate, so that she can enjoy life as she was meant to.

CHAPTER SIX

When Physical or Emotional Health is Disrupted

Death & Mortality, Illness & Injury, Addiction & Recovery

There's an old saying, "If you've got your health you've got everything." While life usually seems a little more complicated than that, it's hard to argue with the basic premise. When we're physically and emotionally healthy, everything else seems to fall into place. Even when it doesn't, we're able to handle the bumps in the road with equanimity.

For many of your clients, though, physical and emotional health aren't always what we'd like them to be. Loved ones get old and die, illness or injury threatens their lives and livelihood, or the pressures of life push them into addiction. Without a strong sense of self-worth and an above average ability to understand and express their emotions, many will find themselves struggling in every area of their lives. Your ability to recognize the loss at the center of their troubles will help them sort through difficult emotions and find the strength to move beyond the challenges that are a part of every life.

Death & Mortality

The death of a loved one is often the first thing that comes to mind in any consideration of loss. I think we can safely say that the most tragic loss for anyone is the death of a parent or child. But the death of a sibling or extended family member or a valued friend or mentor can also be devastating. Even the death of a loved animal companion may be traumatic, as the relationship with a dog or cat, horse, or bird may have provided an unfettered connection, mutual unconditional acceptance, as well as joyful companionship. The loss of any of these relationships can have a powerful and lasting impact on the life of a client, and merits careful attention as you explore the reasons for her current difficulties.

Death also enters the picture when an adult begins to contemplate her mortality. A serious illness or injury, the death of a parent or friend, or the simple changes that come with age may bring her face to face with the reality that she'll one day face her own death. Celebrating a milestone birthday (the sixtieth is often a turning point), entering menopause (or, for a man, andropause), or becoming a grandparent can all force the realization that she is entering her elder years. For some people this recognition is a source of wonder, and fosters a deepening of spirituality and wisdom. But for many it's quite simply terrifying, and can lead to anxiety and depression. Exploring the meaning of one's own mortality can be a very difficult and painful process, but also one of the most rewarding journeys you'll shepherd as a therapist.

As with any loss, the key to moving through the death of a loved one is the ability to freely acknowledge and express the attending emotions. Sadly, there are a variety of reasons why many of us use denial and repression to bury those feelings instead. The most obvious reason is simple pain avoidance. As a matter of self-protection from excruciating pain, many people deny the severity of the loss or repress the accompanying emotions.

Often there are also cultural norms within a family that do not allow for free expression of emotions, particularly negative ones. Husbands, wives, and partners may feel equally compelled to remain "strong" for other family members. In some cases parents are not equipped to express their own emotions, and overtly or covertly teach their children not to express theirs. Even in the healthiest of circumstances, when a death occurs within the family unit a parent might be too overwhelmed with her own grief to be able to effectively assist a child with his. Or she may simply be unaware that her child is silently stricken with pain and confusion that's larger and more complex than he can comprehend, let alone express. And depending on the family dynamic, a sensitive child may feel a responsibility to remain strong in an effort to support a grieving parent.

Society, too, exerts its own pressure to keep feelings under wraps. In the days when rituals such as wakes and funerals are going on, we're allowed some leeway for grieving openly. But soon after, there's an expectation that we'll carry on with work and responsibilities, without burdening others with our tears and sadness. Although death is part of every life, our culture has a particular taboo against speaking about it. Accordingly, friends and co-workers are often at a loss as to what to say or how to treat someone grieving the death of a loved one. And if that loved one happens to have been an animal family member, they may not understand how severe the loss can be, and even ridicule someone who is suffering as a result. It's only natural, then, for someone who is grieving to take the cues to repress her pain, put on a smile—or at least a stiff upper lip—and carry on as if everything is just fine.

The drive to repress the painful emotions may be compounded if your client feels responsible for the death of his loved one. Even if there's no rational justification for it, he may believe the death could have been avoided if he'd been more careful or more observant or more…something. I once worked with a twenty-eight-year-old man named Mike who had lost his wife in a car crash. The morning of the accident his wife had asked him to drop her off at work on his way to a meeting. He'd felt rushed, and told her he was sorry but didn't have time. Afterward he was left with the haunting thought, "If only I had, she wouldn't have." It had been nearly a year since his wife's death, but Mike was still unable to accept his loss because he felt responsible for it, and the notion that he may have somehow caused her accident was just too horrific for him to bear. He buried his feelings where neither he, his friends, nor anyone else could touch them, which made it impossible for him to move successfully through his grieving process. When he finally came to see me his life was falling apart. He had begun to call in sick at work and isolate from friends, and found himself having wine every evening "to help him sleep." Sadly, Mike's case is not unusual. But as long as feelings of guilt or responsibility for the death make the loss too difficult to bear, denial and repression will likely be your client's default coping strategy.

Illness & Injury

Life-threatening or life-altering illness or injury can strike at any time, at any age, and affect the life of not only the patient but of everyone in his sphere of family and friends. Cancer and heart disease are well known to be on the rise in recent decades, with new diagnoses affecting more than three million households every year.[1,2] The long, slow deterioration from diseases of aging, such as Alzheimer's, Parkinson's, or dementia, can debilitate families for years on end. Even the healthiest individuals can be immobilized by an accident that threatens their lives or their ability to function independently.

Mental illness, characterized as any pronounced or prolonged alteration in thinking, mood, or behavior, can be every bit as devastating as physical illness—and it's more common than most people think. According to the National Institute of Mental Health, an estimated one in four Americans may be diagnosed as experiencing some

---

[1] "Estimated New Cancer Cases and Deaths by Sex, US, 2010," American Cancer Society, http://www.cancer.org/Research/CancerFactsFigures/CancerFactsFigures/most-requested-tables-figures-2010.

[2] "Heart Attack and Angina Statistics," American Heart Association, http://www.americanheart.org/presenter.jhtml?identifier=4591.

form of mental disorder in any given year, while nearly half will be affected at some time during their lifetimes.[3] Common disorders such as depression and anxiety, as well as bipolar and other major disorders, typically cause chronic or long-term impairments that range from moderate to disabling in nature. Like most physical illness, mental illness is treatable, and professional help in the form of counseling or medication or both can lead to recovery or successful ongoing management of the condition.

We can't give serious consideration to physical or mental health—or the lack thereof—and ignore the patients' and their families' emotional relationship to it. Severe illness and injury place many different kinds of demands on everyone involved. Aside from the obvious difficulties, such as physical incapacity, the way people think about the infirmity may present the greatest challenge of all. While some readily make the necessary adjustments to habits and lifestyle to accommodate the disability, others view it as a source of shame or resentment, or new evidence of a lack of personal value. As with other types of loss, the response depends to a great extent on how well the individual processes emotions, and the strength of his innate sense of self-worth.

Harold was a forty-one-year-old schoolteacher who had been healthy all of his life. He enjoyed gardening, spending time with

---

[3] National Institute of Mental Health, "Statistics: Any Disorder Among Adults: Prevalence." http://www.nimh.nih.gov/statistics/1ANYDIS_ADULT.shtml.

his children, and playing golf with his wife and friends on the weekend.

While jogging one day, he inadvertently slipped on some gravel and fell on his back. At first he didn't think he was seriously injured, but within a short time he was rushed to the hospital with excruciating pain in his back. It turned out he had ruptured two disks. Initially he believed that with physical therapy and exercise he would soon be back to his old self, playing catch and soccer with son and daughter. This wasn't the case. It was several months before his injury healed enough for him to return to work. In fact, he never fully healed. His back injury prohibited him from enjoying the simplest of pleasures, such as picking up his five-year-old daughter or taking the family's Christmas decorations down from the attic. As his pain and immobility lingered, Harold became quite depressed, which put a strain on his relationship with his wife. It affected his children, too.

In therapy Harold began to recognize his injury as the loss it was, and to identify the many ancillary losses that came with it. Once he was able to grieve those losses he was able to make the adjustments necessary to accommodate his disability. His relationship with his wife stabilized and he began to enjoy his family once again. Although he was unable to play soccer or other athletics with his children, he introduced them to bird watching, a hobby he'd enjoyed in high school but abandoned in college. He also developed a new routine of taking regular long walks with his wife and friends.

Addiction & Recovery

Many of us live with constant anxiety and emotional pain just below the surface. If the pain is always there, anything that makes it go away for a few hours is welcome. For those who turn to food or sex or alcohol, the impulse may be almost totally unconscious. It's as if they've been given a miraculous way out of the struggle. "Now I can cope!" This is an unfortunate solution, but one that's understandable—and easy to come by. In fact, it's not unusual to find that a client struggling with a lifelong addiction began coping in this way as a teenager.

Historically, addiction has been defined solely with regard to psychoactive substances like alcohol, drugs, and tobacco, which all temporarily alter the brain chemically. We now know that it's also possible to become psychologically dependent on things like work and shopping. Spending countless hours on the job is socially acceptable, even admired, and there's a tendency to discount the addictive allure of work as a form of stress relief. When it becomes a compulsive distraction from the pressures of life or unresolved emotions too painful to face, work itself can become an addiction. Similarly, shopping is normally an innocuous and even necessary behavior. But when it becomes compulsive, the cost becomes clear when the credit card bills come due.

Indeed, the list of potentially addictive objects and behaviors is seemingly limitless, and includes such things as food, gambling, sex, computers, video games, the internet, pornography, exercise, and watching television, just to name a few. While these behaviors don't directly introduce chemicals into the body, they may trigger the release of chemicals such as endorphins that generate feelings of pleasure or relaxation—temporarily. In all cases they serve as a distraction from pain and suffering, and become part of the denial mechanism that prevents the sufferer from dealing with difficult emotions.

Whatever the behavior, it counts as an addiction when it becomes obsessive and interferes with the normal activities, relationships, and responsibilities of everyday life. As a result, succumbing to it can lead to guilt, shame, fear, hopelessness, failure, rejection, anxiety, and depression. Addictive behavior is maladaptive or counterproductive to the individual, often undermining his ability to overcome other problems or adapt to difficult situations. Still, he continues to engage in the behavior even though it causes trouble for him. A sex addict may crave intimacy, yet the focus on sexual acts may prevent real closeness from developing. A drinker might want to cheer herself up, yet alcohol actually contributes to the development of depression. When people are addicted their attention and energy become focused on carrying out the addictive behavior rather than on enjoying the full range of experiences that shape their potential for happiness.

The risks of succumbing to an addiction have no socioeconomic or racial boundaries. Individuals from upper- and middle-class backgrounds are just as much at risk as are those living in poverty. The primary difference lies in the tendency of caregivers to overlook or even forgive addictive behavior in the upper- or middle-class person. You'll want to make it a priority, then, to understand the indicators and dynamics of this disorder, and probe for it when treating every client.

All forms of addiction contain a psychological component. Successful therapy can clarify the psychological issues and help a client understand more clearly the nature of her cravings and self-destructive behaviors. This insight proves invaluable as she begins to adopt healthier ways of coping with life's challenges and painful emotions. With your support she'll be able to develop new patterns of behavior that will not only be more appropriate, but that will support her in her attempt to recover from her addictions and become whole again.

What Is Lost?

What exactly is lost when a loved one dies?

It may seem like a silly question with an obvious answer: "I lost someone I loved!"

True enough. However, the healing process begins when you help your client understand the meaning of that loss in the most personal terms. To do that you'll need to be conscious of exactly how her world changed when the death occurred. You'll examine her relationship with the deceased and the ways she was nurtured by it. If he was a financial provider, the reality of economic loss will require attention. And if he was a significant presence in her daily life, chances are her routines, her lifestyle, and possibly her social network will have changed.

The same is true when a loved one is severely ill or injured or struggling with an addiction. In every case, you'll find that more is lost than the initial death, illness, or drink would suggest. As you examine the many things that were lost as a result of the initial crisis, you'll be able to help your client grieve those losses and move toward acceptance and healing. Here are a few things she may have suddenly found missing:

- The comfort and security of the consistent presence of a loved one, doing all the things he used to do
- Loving companionship
- The support and encouragement of someone who knew her very well
- The joy of having someone to share special moments
- The presence of someone who called forth powerful feelings of love in her heart
- The loss of dreams, hopes, and plans
- Financial security
- Emotional safety or security
- Unconditional love
- A sense of knowing what to expect from the world
- A deep, soul connection unlike any other
- The support of a partner who can help carry the load of maintaining a home and family

If your client is dealing with his own mortality, illness, injury, or addiction, he'll be struggling to come to terms with the ways his life is not what it used to be, or not what he hoped it would be. Even the normal aging process brings the loss of the young, nimble body that was once capable of doing most anything he asked of it. In the case of devastating illnesses such as cancer or organ failure, the patient may lose a body part—a breast, a uterus, a kidney—all losses that are akin to a personal death, and that must be grieved like any other traumatic loss.

Here are some of the things your ill, injured, or addicted client may have lost:

- His independence
- The ability to function as he did in the past
- The ability to take care of himself physically or financially
- His sense of value as a spouse or parent
- His sense of security
- The opportunity to experience many of the simple pleasures he used to enjoy
- The ability to be a productive member of the family or workplace
- Control over his body, his environment, and his life
- The joy of being able to spontaneously interact and engage with the outside world
- The ability to participate in sports and other physically demanding recreational activities
- The belief that he is attractive to his partner
- Self-esteem
- His job
- His home
- The respect and support of others

- Quality of life
- A reliable companion, even if that companion was a destructive substance or behavior (as for the recovering addict)
- The illusion that life as he knows it will go on forever

The Long-Term Impact

The various pressures to avoid dealing with a disruption in one's own health or that of a loved one are potent, but the consequences of yielding to that pressure can be severe. When we're unable to express our pain, it follows us and stays in our souls—or, in psychotherapeutic terms, it remains buried in the unconscious mind. It interferes with the ability to feel emotions of all kinds, and could hamper the ability to form intimate, lasting relationships. Repressing emotions also inevitably causes a great deal of stress, which adversely affects physical health as well.

When a loved one's health is disrupted

This pattern of repression often begins at an early age, as a result of either overt pressure from significant adults or the example they covertly set as they stifle their own emotions. Consider a child dealing with the death of a parent—quite possibly the worst thing that can happen to a child. It is an unbearable loss that, if not grieved, will haunt him throughout his life. It is especially difficult for a young child to understand the concept of death, and often takes some time for this loss to register in a substantive, permanent way.

It's particularly confusing when the pain of loss is mingled with inevitable feelings of anger. Whether the one who has died is a parent, grandparent, sibling, or other significant figure, death often feels like abandonment to a child. He may feel angry or resentful, which in turn triggers feelings of guilt. It's easy to see why this complicated array of emotions may not get resolved to completion until many years later.

It stands to reason, then, that for a child the death of a loved one is confusing and bewildering at best. Without a great deal of support and encouragement from significant adults he may never find the bridge between grasping the magnitude of the loss and expressing the pain and anger it caused, and he's unlikely to resolve his latent feelings of guilt or responsibility for the death, or learn to live successfully without his beloved parent. That's why so many adults who lost loved ones as children still carry the burden of the original trauma.

Serious physical or mental illness or addiction in a parent can also be extremely confusing for a child. When Mommy or Daddy is not able to nurture or care for him, from the child's perspective it's a form of emotional neglect, even if the parent is unavailable through no choice of her own. If other significant adults are not able to help the youngster understand what's happening and process his grief, confusion, and fears, his innate sense of safety, trust, and self-worth will be compromised, and the unresolved emotions will impact his relationships indefinitely.

When the loss of a loved one occurs during adulthood, it's reasonable to assume a healthy adult will have developed coping skills that will enable him to find the strength to experience the depth of his pain, express it in the company of supportive friends and family members, and release it. When that happens the grieving process can unfold naturally and, in time, acceptance and healing will occur. If, however, he never learned as a child to express his emotions, or to identify his needs and get them met, he'll be unable to benefit from the healing that comes from sharing his feelings with loved ones and receiving their support. If an adult client comes to you for assistance dealing with a death or illness that occurred in recent time, it's safe to assume there is another, older loss lurking beneath the surface, and the buried pain, anger, and resentment of the earlier trauma has come flooding back. Loss begets loss, and the compounded emotions of the two or more traumatic events may prove more than he can manage without professional assistance. Or perhaps life has simply taught him to devalue his emotional life in favor of elevating the importance of his intellectual life, and so he doggedly takes a rational approach to his loss, casting his feelings aside as irrelevant. If societal pressures or family responsibilities cause him to repress his emotions, the grieving process may be stifled. Any of these circumstances can leave your client feeling depressed or anxious, or having difficulty feeling emotions of any kind. His relationships may also suffer.

Many people do not realize that the loss of a parent is a major life event at any age—even when it occurs during adulthood. Relationships with siblings are particularly vulnerable to the dynamics that play out when a mother or father becomes seriously ill or dies. Prior issues between brothers and sisters can emerge or worsen. Jealousy and envy, particularly in the context of parental favoritism, will rear their ugly heads. Changing roles among family members are inevitable, as when the disabled or deceased parent was the one who was the "glue" in the family keeping other members together, or the holder of the family secrets. These are just a few of the strains that will affect siblings' ability to cope with an already difficult situation. Unless family members are able to get clear about their anger and sadness, and adjust to the new responsibilities that might arise due to the loss in the family, there may be a whole new raft of emotions that are at risk of being repressed.

Often the illness or death of a loved one—or even a casual friend—affects us in ways we may not expect. That was my client Sophie's experience.

Sophie was fifty-five years old when we met, and had been suffering from panic attacks that had increased in frequency and severity over the prior six months. She had two grown daughters who lived a couple of hours away, and described her relationship with her spouse as compatible and supportive. She enjoyed working as a pediatric nurse, and also played tennis weekly with a friend. When we began to talk about her experiences in the previous year, she revealed that one of her dearest childhood friends had, after a long battle, succumbed to cancer.

We explored Sophie's response to the death of her friend, and it soon became apparent that the experience had triggered Sophie's fear of her own mortality. As we continued to investigate her fears she was able to get in touch with the many losses that had occurred during her lifetime, and the realization that she'd "never had time to think about them" because "life was hectic."

Sophie came to understand that, with her friend's passing, her own mortality had become more of a reality to her than it had ever been before. She began to realize she had a long list of buried dreams and desires, and feared that, like her friend, she might not get the chance to fulfill them. We spent several months talking about the death of Sophie's friend and allowing Sophie the time and space she needed to grieve. She also mourned her "lost years"—the dreams she hadn't pursued, the risks she'd never taken, and the realization that more than half of her life was over. As the months wore on Sophie mourned for those she loved who had died and for the fragility of her own life. In time, her panic attacks vanished.

When the reality of one's own mortality suddenly looms large, fear is often the result, as it was for Sophie. Others find themselves depressed, or withdrawing from family and friends—particularly those who are much older or younger, because they are vivid reminders of the aging process. Some clients engage in self-destructive behaviors, as though attempting to stare death in the face.

When your client is the patient

When we're healthy we take for granted the ability to grab a purse or wallet and head out to the store for a simple errand or to meet a friend for lunch. When one is disabled due to injury or illness, this is not always possible. Getting ready can take planning, and perhaps even the support of a caregiver. The otherwise benign act of leaving the home environment, where one feels secure, can elicit anxiety.

If your client is the one dealing with physical or mental illness, the impact is real and unavoidable. He may be able to repress early trauma with the complex power of his mind. But health issues cannot be repressed. He is forced to cope with the limitations of his illness, which always come with emotional unrest. Feelings of vulnerability, insecurity, and inadequacy are likely to surface.

Whether it be cancer, diabetes, multiple sclerosis, epilepsy, depression, or any other debilitating illness, the presence or absence of a solid support network will determine the degree to which he is able to function within the limitations of his condition. If support is not available, he will have difficulty communicating his distress and his need for help. He is likely to isolate himself, which is likely to lead to depression. As depression deepens he'll lose interest in himself and others and develop a sense of loneliness, frustration, and hopelessness. He may stop taking care of himself, start self-medicating with drugs or alcohol, or fail to follow through with proper medical care and treatment—which can lead to a worsening of his condition or even an early death.

When addiction is the illness, the consequences are similar—but with a twist. In addiction and recovery we find an interesting cycle in our study of loss. Drugs, alcohol, work, shopping, and other addictions are often a consequence of unresolved loss, because they tend to numb the pain of emotions that seem too difficult to face. But because they're so destructive they generate a whole new set of losses—for the addicted individual and also for her loved ones. Health, financial stability, relationships, employment, and self-esteem may all be compromised. To complete the cycle, when the sufferer does begin recovery from addiction, she may experience giving up the destructive substance or behavior as a loss. After all, her drug of choice has been a "friend" that has been with her through tough times. It even made her pain go away—temporarily, at least. As she regains her health she'll recognize that the cost was far too great.

Indeed, the impact of addiction is far-reaching and terribly destructive to your client's quality of life. Substance abuse and obsessive behaviors interfere with her ability to perform the day-to-day functions that keep a home and a job intact. It's likely she'll fail to fulfill her responsibilities, and disappoint loved ones again and again and again. Her demeanor may become antagonistic, disruptive, sullen, withdrawn, or erratic. Her financial situation can deteriorate due to the cost of paying for her drugs or shopping or gambling, or simply because she can no longer generate income. Primary relationships might fail, and family and friends become estranged. As her life crumbles around her she'll experience shame, loss of self-respect, and depression.

Recovery from addiction is a long and challenging process. When your client begins to take stock of the consequences of her addiction she'll feel regret and disappointment for what could have been: lost time, lost opportunities, lost loved ones. Shame and loss of self-respect can be overwhelming, and often threaten to send the patient back to her addiction to numb her pain.

Presenting Symptoms

Many people come to therapy because they are having various relationship difficulties, or because they are dissatisfied with life; they feel deadened and don't know why. These concerns are often the catalyst that brings them to deal at last with unresolved losses. Death, health issues, and addiction frequently emerge as losses that need to be addressed.

Once you begin inviting your client to talk about a disruption in physical or emotional health, listen closely to the way he describes that loss. The language he uses will provide valuable clues to his innermost thoughts and feelings, and learning to notice those clues is one of the most critical tools available to you. When someone is struggling to distance himself from a painful experience or minimize its effect, that effort will inevitably be reflected in his choice of words. Phrases like, "I was so young, I didn't really know my mother," or, "Granddad was so old, it was his time," are simply masks designed to hide the very real emotions those deaths brought about. Similarly, euphemisms such as "He passed on," or "He's gone to a better place," may reflect your client's true beliefs about what happens to the spirit when the physical body dies—or they may be a way to avoid saying the unbearable truth, "He died." Making light of a life-threatening illness—his own or that of a loved one—may also indicate there's more going on than he realizes.

Here are some of the presenting symptoms that may indicate your client is suffering the impact of unresolved emotions from a loss of physical or emotional health:

- Difficulties in relationships
- A lack of close, intimate relationships
- A tendency to be closed off emotionally, from himself and from others
- Difficulty trusting himself and others
- A pattern of sabotaging relationships
- Generalized malaise, or dissatisfaction with life
- Difficulty feeling emotions, or a "dead" feeling inside
- An irrational, ongoing fear that an otherwise healthy relationship will end
- Frequent feelings of betrayal or blame
- An inability to form strong attachments
- Panic attacks, anxiety, or depression
- Physical symptoms such as headaches, heart disease, problems in the digestive tract (ulcers, colitis), insomnia
- Euphemistic language that dismisses the severity of the loss
- Difficulty getting over the end of a relationship
- Self-destructive behavior

Recognizing symptoms of addiction requires a particularly watchful eye, because the signs are not always easy to detect. Some clients exhibit clear signs that will put you on alert. Others hide their addiction very well, and it could take weeks or months before you suspect a problem.

Lessons in Loss

Following are some of the behaviors you can recognize as warning signs that your client may in fact be an addict:

- Moodiness or irritability
- Depression
- Mood swings
- Reports or evidence of personality changes or inconsistent behaviors
- Self-defeating behaviors, such as absence from work, missed appointments, tardiness
- Reports or evidence of withdrawal symptoms when the addictive substance or behavior is not available to her
- Reports of broken friendships, with confusion regarding the reason
- Unwillingness to take responsibility for the consequences of her behavior
- Defiance
- Blaming others for her troubles
- Reports of repetitive behavior or excessive participation in a particular activity
- Coming to appointments under the influence of drugs or alcohol
- Rapid weight loss or gain
- Changes in physical appearance or personal hygiene

- Reports of frequently neglected responsibilities at home or at work
- High-risk behaviors

✦ ✦ ✦

Every client must cope with death, illness, or injury—their own or that of a loved one—at some point in life. Not everyone has a direct encounter with addiction, but many teeter on the brink as they struggle to cope with unresolved loss, and some will fall into the abyss. Exploring the ways disruptions in health have affected your client should be part of every assessment. Helping her understand and accept those losses will enable her to develop healthy coping strategies, and be better prepared to support loved ones when they need it most.

CHAPTER SEVEN

The Many Faces of Loss

Loss of a Job, Life Changes, Trauma, and More

So far we've examined some of the most common and devastating types of loss your clients have experienced. But loss wears many, many faces, and the more adept you become at recognizing it wherever and however it appears, the more easily you'll be able to help your clients identify the traumas underlying the difficulties that brought them to your office.

In this chapter you'll find an overview of life's challenging events, what your clients may have lost as a result, and the impact if the loss remains unresolved.

The Loss of a Job

Whether your client quit his job or was fired or laid off, finding himself unemployed can be unsettling to his identity. Men in particular tend to identify with their work. It's not just what they do, but who they are. Not having a job to go to or a paycheck to bring home can leave him feeling like a failure as a provider and as a man. For men and women alike, uncertainty about how they'll provide for themselves and their families can deal a severe blow to self-esteem. The loss of financial stability, identity, and sense of self-worth can lead to anxiety and depression. He may lose the friends he associated with at work and his standing in the community. His relationship with his spouse and children may suffer, and in his frustration he may become sullen, irritable, or abusive. He might even turn to substance abuse. If the lack of income persists, he may lose his home, his quality of life—even his family.

The loss of a home

A home is a safe haven, the place we go to retreat from the busy-ness and uncertainties of "the world out there." We decorate it to reflect who we are, and fill it with comforts and memorabilia that make it our own. But foreclosure, eviction, fire or flood, or a variety of other circumstances can force your client out of her home. Her sense of safety and security may be shaken, particularly if older unresolved issues of loss have left her with poorly developed sense of security and ability to trust. Chances are she'll also lose the companionship and support of neighbors and friends who live nearby. While going to the mailbox or bringing in the newspaper, gardening or shoveling snow, or simply heading out in the morning and coming home at the end of the day, those familiar faces provide a sense of stability. While relationships with those folks may not be intimate, they make us feel part of a community. When all of these comforts are gone due to the loss of a home, your client may become withdrawn, isolated, anxious, or depressed.

Moving

Even when the move is voluntary, and your client is moving to a new place she loves, the loss of a familiar house and home can be unsettling for all the reasons we explored above. While the impact is likely to be less severe than a forced move, it's important to recognize this event as a loss, and explore the feelings that arise as a result.

A child's first day of school

Even the most positive events can be stressful. While heading off for that first day of school is a happy and necessary step, it can be difficult for parents as well as the child. Both experience a level of separation from one another that's unprecedented. The child must adjust to a new schedule, a new school, a new teacher, a classroom full of new friends—and with so many changes the stage is set for uncertainty about safety and security. In many cases it's the first time he'll be separated from his primary caregiver for so much of his day—day after day after day. The separation from that special love and care that only a parent can provide will test his basic sense of trust in the world.

For the parents, placing their child in the hands of a teacher may feel like a loss of control over the child's education and safety. They'll lose that sense that they are the sole significant adults in his life, which may trigger insecurity and uncertainty about their self-worth. And of course, there's sadness about not having the little one around for part of the day, and a need to grieve the loss of the baby who has grown into a youngster heading off to school.

Going to school marks the first of many passages parents and children will experience as they grow toward independence. It has symbolic meaning for everyone, just like the first steps a toddler takes on his own. We often see a child having a difficult time leaving his mother or father on the first days of school, only to discover that the separation anxiety has more to do with the parents' fears and anxieties at losing their child than the with his fears of leaving home. Inevitably he'll pick up on his parent's anxieties, which is why it often appears that it is the child that is having a difficult time separating and not the parent.

It's essential for parents to acknowledge their grief and uncertainty at a time like this. It may be of value to revisit your client's experience with her own first day of school, and discover whether there are unresolved issues of loss from that early experience of separation and change.

Bullying

The degree to which bullying has become commonplace in our schools is truly troubling. But in truth, the problem is not new. Children have been intimidating and harassing one another for as long as they've been playing together. Sadly, the problem is not unique to the schoolyard or the playground. It is not uncommon for older siblings or cousins to bully children at home. With so much potential for trouble, there's a reasonable chance your client has experienced it at some point in his history.

When a child is bullying another child, invariably he's also a victim of a bully. Of course, parents are actually the biggest culprits, and they often do not realize the harmful effects their boorish behavior has on their children. When a youngster is ridiculed—by his peers or his parents—it damages his self-esteem, his sense of trust, and his belief that he has value in the world. In an effort to avoid attracting the attention of others who might ridicule him he may spend the rest of his life withdrawn or not living up to his potential. Or he may go to inordinate lengths to prove himself worthy through perfectionism, workaholism, or setting ever higher goals for himself and never feeling "good enough."

Recognizing a history of being bullied as an unresolved loss, and expressing the pain, fear, and isolation he felt as a result, will help your client reclaim his self-esteem and achieve a greater sense of ease and peace. It's also a critical step in breaking a cycle that might otherwise perpetuate itself.

A best friend moves away

Close friendships are a key source of emotional support, often as significant as family—or more so. The loss of a best friend, even if only because she moves to another town, can feel like a death. It's easy for other friends and family members to discount the importance of this kind of loss, but your client will need to acknowledge it and grieve, much as she would grieve a death or a divorce. It's also worthwhile to be on the lookout for a similar experience that may have occurred during her childhood, but that may have been discounted by parents or other significant adults.

The empty nest

When the kids finally go off on their own, whether to college, a first apartment, or to be married, it can be tough rattling around a big empty house. Suddenly a parent's job is over—or so it may seem—and the sense of value that comes from having someone to look after is lost. It is not uncommon for a marriage to fall apart once the children have moved out, particularly if the couple has grown apart because they failed to nurture their romantic relationship over the years, allowing child rearing to become their primary bond.

It's important to ensure that your client acknowledges the grief that may come as a result of an empty nest, and recognizes the many other ways she still has value in the world. If she's married, you'll also want to help her explore ways to rekindle her romance with her partner and deepen their bond.

Marriage

This is another happy event that is not without stress. The joy of embarking on a new life with a loved and loving partner may obscure the inevitable losses that come with it. A new bride or groom will lose the freedom and independence of being single, as well as favorite activities and familiar routines that must be set aside to accommodate the needs of a spouse and a partnership. Chances are the transition will include a move, and perhaps separation from friends and family members. Sadly there's often disappointment as the new husband or wife discovers that the reality of marriage is a far cry from the fairytale he or she had imagined it would be. All of these losses must be acknowledged and grieved, or they may sow the seeds of resentment that can cloud the marriage for years to come.

Puberty

Like the first day of school, puberty is a milestone that signals a healthy transition toward adulthood, but that can bring with it feelings of loss. Of course, when a flood of hormones is part of the picture, all manner of confusing emotions and conflicting needs and desires make the adjustment all the more complicated. In addition, there's the potential for embarrassment and ridicule by peers as a young body changes and the adolescent struggles to learn to manage and express his sexuality in appropriate ways.

If your client is having difficulty with self-esteem, with trust, or expressing his sexuality, spend some time investigating his experience with puberty, and if necessary help him explore any related unresolved issues of loss that may be lingering.

Menopause and andropause

Menopause is widely understood to be a potentially challenging time for a woman as fluctuations in her hormones cause a loss of fertility and an array of physical and emotional changes. Far less attention has been given to the hormonal changes men experience as they age. The reduction in testosterone in males is far more gradual than the reduction of estrogen in females, so for many men the changes are more subtle and more easily accommodated. But some struggle with noticeable changes in their bodies and their emotions, and while men remain fertile into old age their ability to perform sexually may diminish. In addition to the physical and emotional changes, both menopause and andropause are signs that time is marching on, and women and men alike may fear the loss of their youth and feel less attractive sexually. Your assistance in recognizing the signs—in your male and your female clients—will help them adjust to those changes and move through the transition without the burden of unresolved issues of loss.

Aging

Some people begin to struggle with the losses that come with aging while still in their thirties, or younger. Others become fearful or anxious as menopause or andropause sets in, or when the first wrinkles or grey hairs appear. Still others glide easily through life's changes until a decline in physical health makes it difficult for them to function as they would like to.

As your client begins to face the steady march of time, she may find herself mourning for opportunities missed and experiences she'll never have. These regrets might include not having a loving and nurturing childhood, a love interest she never pursued or one she had and lost, unrequited love, or choosing a job that was safe instead of pursuing her passion. Or it might be as simple (yet far-reaching) as not sharing her feelings of love more openly with her family or friends.

Whenever the effects of aging make their presence known, and whatever form they take, your client will benefit from a willingness to grieve the loss of a youthful body, and an ability to recognize the emotions that arise in response, so she can make the transition to her elder years with grace, wisdom, and joy.

Burglary or robbery

A direct, unwelcome invasion of personal boundaries is always traumatic. A burglary or robbery may involve the loss of property, but more significant is the loss of a sense of personal safety and trust. A violation of this kind is likely to trigger any latent fears or insecurities, and is fertile ground for exploring unresolved issues of loss due to compromised boundaries, such as physical or sexual abuse. Whether or not your client has a history of abuse, in the face of any personal attack anger, confusion, fear, and anxiety are likely to emerge—if they're allowed to. He may be inclined to dismiss the violation as insignificant, but be sure to provide ample opportunity and support for him to revisit and release any repressed emotions surrounding his basic sense of safety.

Rape

Like sexual abuse, rape is one of the most invasive violations a woman—or a man—can endure. Whether the event is a violent encounter with a stranger, undue pressure from a friend, a date, or a spouse, or anything in between, the damage to the victim's sense of self is profound. Fear, anger, anxiety, shame, and guilt may stir, and her sense of self-worth, safety, and trust in the world may all be lost. It's essential that your client receive all the support she needs to thoroughly explore and express the complex and powerful emotions she'll experience, or the event will haunt her for the rest of her life.

✦ ✦ ✦

It's clear that any and all of the challenges your clients face as they make their way in the world are potentially experiences of loss. This list is by no means comprehensive. But my hope is that it will help you exercise your muscles of observation, so that you become skillful at recognizing the potential for loss that lies within the various stories your clients will bring to you. With your growing understanding of what exactly is lost in the joys and sorrows of every life, you can help them recover their losses and move forward on the path of healing.

Part Three

The Solutions

CHAPTER EIGHT

Treatment Strategies for Healing Unresolved Loss

Now that you have a solid understanding of the many ways loss has impacted the lives of your clients and the reasons they come to you for treatment, it's time to explore how that knowledge will inform your approach to therapy. Your goal is to help them explore the unresolved losses that interfere with their ability to function at their best, and that undermine their quality of life.

As we've seen, the emotions associated with those old, unresolved traumas are often buried beneath years of denial and repression because they were simply too painful to bear when they first arose. But in the context of the safe and supportive environment you'll create, and with your compassionate and skillful approach to treatment, your clients will find the courage to revisit those traumas and experience the full range of emotions that go with them, so they can realize their potential for the rich and rewarding lives they deserve.

Create a Space for Healing

The physical environment in which you conduct your practice sets the tone for the work you and your client will do together. It's the first thing she'll experience when she arrives at her sessions, and creates a backdrop for how she'll feel when she's in your office. Taking the time to create an environment that reflects the safe, supportive therapeutic relationship she'll need is a sound investment in the quality of treatment you can provide.

Location, location, location

Although there are many factors you'll take into consideration when deciding on a location for your office, it has been my experience that choosing a safe neighborhood is essential. If your client feels uneasy before she walks in the door, she'll have one more obstacle to overcome before she can let her guard down and explore the inner world that feels unsafe. A quiet, nonthreatening locale will help her feel at ease.

It makes sense, too, to choose a location that's easy to get to, with convenient parking. If your office is in a city, it will be helpful if it's accessible via public transportation. The more you can do to keep the process of getting to therapy easy, the more likely it is your clients will be in a peaceful, open frame of mind when they arrive.

Choosing a neighborhood where other therapists practice is also a plus for you as well as your clients. They may find it reassuring to know that other folks are going through similar experiences, particularly when they leave your office in tears or feeling vulnerable. You'll appreciate the sense of community that comes from having other therapists nearby to consult with or simply share a lunch break.

Some therapists choose to have their offices in their homes. Before you make that choice, be aware that it would mean exposing a part of your private life to your clients, and be certain you're comfortable doing that. Keep in mind that your clients will have many feelings and thoughts about you (including envy, if they perceive your house or your neighborhood as nicer than theirs), and will project some of their difficult emotions onto you. I remember seeing a client who had previously been in therapy with someone who had an office in her house. The client would hear the therapist's children running through the house, and on a couple of occasions saw her husband entering and leaving the house. She felt jealous and intruded upon, but was unable to discuss her feelings with the therapist. One of the losses she was working to heal was the emotional abuse and neglect she'd experienced as a child. She longed for a mother who would be attentive and caring, and projected that longing onto her therapist. She was also aware of the fact that she couldn't afford to live in a house like her therapist's home. She often left her sessions feeling left out, unimportant, and of little value in the world—just as she'd felt as a child. Eventually her various responses to the home office became too confusing and overwhelming, and she felt she needed to terminate the therapy.

The lesson here is that under any circumstances there will be projections and fantasies and imaginings about who you are and how you live. It's inevitable that your office environment will feed your clients' projections and imagination. Keep it warm and inviting, but be mindful regarding the amount of personal information it conveys about you.

Your waiting room

The waiting area outside your office should be clean, comfortable, and well lit, but not overly stimulating. It should convey the idea that you care about your clients' comfort, and that you take yourself seriously as a professional. Your choice of magazines also deserves careful consideration. They provide your clients with something to do while waiting, and give them a natural distraction from others in the waiting room. In most social settings folks might naturally address each other in such close quarters. But when going to therapy most people prefer privacy, and do not wish to be put in a position of needing to make small talk or discuss why they are going to therapy.

Your inner sanctum

The space where you do your healing work should be tranquil and welcoming, and invite your clients to "curl up on the couch, kick your shoes off, and talk!!!" It has been my experience that when choosing art, furniture, and personal belongings for our offices, we need to consider the effect it will have on our clients. If we want them to fully bring themselves to the therapy, then I think it is important to make room *for them*. For example, you might like modern furniture, but will that furniture be comfortable for a client to sit in? Will they feel calm and peaceful when they walk into your room? Or will a big overstuffed couch put them more at ease?

I also believe it is good form to shut off your telephone, cell phone, pager, and computer so your client has your undivided attention. A phone that rings when she's about to share something she's never told anyone before is intrusive, disrespectful, and defeating.

Finally, remember to keep an ample supply of kleenex within reach at all times. And of course, don't forget to keep the bathroom well stocked with paper goods.

The Therapeutic Relationship

All of us need relationships to give our lives meaning. Without human contact an infant will not survive or thrive. As adults, our ability to change and grow and heal is rooted in our ability to feel understood and respected by another. The relationship between a client and his therapist is designed to provide that understanding and respect without the complications of a personal relationship.

If the therapy is to be successful, a variety of components must be present for the client in a consistent and reliable way.

- In addition to understanding and respect there must be shared goals for the treatment, based on the client's needs.

- The client needs to feel you are genuinely interested in what he has to say, and in what he feels, needs, and wants. In short, he must feel cared about.
- Your client should be able to count on you to be trustworthy, dependable, consistent, and honest.
- The therapist must establish clear and consistent boundaries (see "Maintain healthy boundaries" on page 122), and clear expectations regarding agreements such as fees and cancellations.
- The healing will be facilitated by an atmosphere that encourages curiosity on the part of the client, and a new way of thinking about his problems, behaviors, needs, wants, and desires. The therapist and client together will take an active interest in why he is the way he is.
- Make it clear that your allegiance is with your client, and that you are not there to judge, persuade, or impose your agenda. Even if you don't agree with what he is doing or what he has done, practice non-judgment. Be empathetic and compassionate.

I believe that each of us knows best what we need and want for our greatest good, but our fears get in the way of our ability to access that expertise. It's of tremendous value to your client if you make it clear that you trust in his ability to know what he needs, and in his ability to change. The therapeutic relationship is much like the parent-child relationship. In both instances a bond needs to be forged to allow the relationship to deepen in trust and dependability so the client can be vulnerable, knowing you will be there to support him.

I like to think the catalyst for all of us becoming therapists is the wish to serve people, and that we have the capacity for deep compassion and empathy. Although there are many theoretical orientations, our inherent compassion and empathy are best expressed in the common denominator of the therapist-client relationship. For many clients it's the first relationship in which they experience the kind of support, acceptance, care, and concern we wish they'd received from their parents.

When children grow up in families where there is open communication, they learn to talk about their problems to people (their parents) who care, which later translates to choosing partners and friends who share this value. Listening, caring, and sharing compassion with another are truly the essential elements that help us move through difficult times in our lives. Too often children grow up in families in which there is no communication of feelings, and they don't get to witness their parents experiencing their own feelings or sorting out their problems with others. Those children learn to shut down their emotional lives, and instead attempt to get through life without the help of others. Even worse, they cut themselves off from their own emotional experience. This is often the main reason people seek out therapy. They know something is missing, but they don't know what it is until they begin to experience it—in the context of the therapeutic relationship. Through that therapeutic relationship we can help our clients begin to talk about their feelings and their struggles, and through role modeling and encouragement we help them reclaim their emotional lives. In turn, they become more aware of their needs and desires and learn how to express them to others.

Establish and maintain trust

We've talked a lot about trust throughout the pages of this book. As we've seen, it's one of the first things that are lost when a child—or an adult—faces a debilitating loss. Overcoming that particular loss is a critical part of the healing process. As a therapist you'll provide a context for your client to explore what it means to be able to trust another human being. It's vital, then, that she learns early on that you are in fact someone she can trust—and that you earn her confidence again with each and every exchange. Here are a few examples of behaviors that signal to your client that you're someone she can trust—*really* trust.

- Be punctual. Beginning and ending sessions on time is reassuring for your client, as it establishes what she can expect at each visit.
- Express a genuine interest, compassion, and a desire to be of help.
- Offer hope. Say things like, "I believe I can be of help to you in learning to understand…."
- Return phone calls in a timely manner.
- Be clear about housekeeping matters—fees, cancellation policy, vacation policy, and so forth.
- Be honest.
- Encourage her to tell you everything on her mind.

- Do your best to remember what your client talks about—anything that's important to her. For example, if in the first session she mentions that the sun is in her eyes while sitting in her chair, it's good form to adjust the blinds to make her more comfortable, and to continue to do so before she arrives for her subsequent visits. Also, thank her for telling you about it. That will help to establish her importance to you, and indicate that her comfort matters.

- There are always issues of power that need to be worked out in any relationship. This is also true in your relationship with your client. You'll need to strike a balance between "I am an expert" and "I don't know everything nor do I have all the answers." Being honest about what you know and what you don't know is part of being someone your client can trust.

- In turn, trust your client. Not only will it model what it means to trust another, but it will also empower her to trust herself.

Overcoming resistance

One of the challenges of therapy—for both the client and the therapist—is the client's resistance. It's frightening to discover the difficult truths about one's life. Doing so allows painful memories to surface, as well as one's own negative feelings such as anger, repulsion, greed, envy, jealousy, hate, and fear. Most folks have a difficult time acknowledging they have such feelings, even though it's perfectly natural to have them. Still, clients put up any number of defenses and obstacles to avoid allowing the truth to surface.

When a client is resistant he is usually protecting himself from facing something that was at one time in his life too threatening to know. You'll find examples of this scenario scattered throughout the pages of this book:

- "I don't want to know that my father was abusive to me...I would rather think of him as a little hotheaded, or that he was trying to teach me right from wrong."
- "I don't want to know my world collapsed when my mother died when I was a child...it's too painful to know I suffered that way."
- "I don't want to know how I neglected my children when I was taking drugs."
- "I don't want to know I felt angry and resentful of my mother when she died of cancer when I was seven years old."

Resistance can take many forms. As your conversation and questions lead your client back to the unresolved loss, his unconscious mind will send a distress signal, and suddenly a wall will go up. He may dismiss the issue as unimportant, abruptly change the subject, or simply become distracted. He might get confused, or literally forget what he was talking about. When your work together begins to close in on issues he's been avoiding for years, he might even begin arriving late for appointments or miss them completely.

Needless to say, it's necessary to overcome resistance if true healing is to occur. How will you do that? The simple answer is, "With understanding and patience." Understand that resistance is nothing more than fear, and that the fear is there for a good reason—it protected your client when he was too fragile or lacked the support to face the truth. His presence in your office is an indication that he's approaching that moment when, with your support, he can face those demons and release them. Help him, encourage him, guide him, and lead him. But have the patience to allow him to move into that painful space in his own time, when he is ready. We all grow emotionally at our own pace, and no two people are alike. As therapists, we never push people past what they are ready to know. There is a fine line between staying with someone and supporting him as he moves into difficult territory, and pushing him into knowing something he is not yet able to handle.

One way to stay on the healthy side of that line is by monitoring the signals you observe, and helping your client tolerate his distress by remaining supportive, open, and responsive to his discomfort. If you sense he's moving too quickly into difficult territory, you can slow things down and give him time to assimilate new information in smaller doses. Here are some tools that will help you do that:

- Help him not to say too much at one time, or more than he can handle.
- Gently interrupt him and check in with him about what he's feeling.

Lessons in Loss

- Ask if he notices any physical sensations. That will help him to stay connected to the present moment, and also teach him to monitor his own emotions.
- You might simply stop him and say, "You know, I want to check something out with you.... I am picking up an uneasiness as you were talking. Might that be right?"

All of this is to say that people often don't know their own limits. They sometimes just blurt things out, become overwhelmed, and then pull away in fear—by putting a halt to the exploration, missing sessions, or even quitting therapy altogether. That's why it's so important to remain attuned to your client's words and body language, invite him to explore those buried feelings, but help him to do it at a pace he can handle. Thus, as he uncovers and resolves the previously unconscious emotions, he'll no longer need to be afraid of what is hidden, and no longer need to act out of fear nor repress his thoughts or feelings or memories. Simply breaking that pattern often leads to immediate and significant life changes, because when we understand one set of defenses—why we have them, what we were hiding from—we can apply that knowledge to other situations in our lives.

The bottom line is this: Know that resistance is a real and powerful factor in any treatment process. Be cautious, be observant, and watch for cues that your client is ready to move forward—or that he's not. In my experience, every client comes to terms with what he needs to know, *if* he stays in therapy. If you push too hard too soon, you may lose him. If you offer patience and understanding within the safe context of your therapeutic relationship, in time the resistance will fall away and he'll be ready to see the truth in all its human messiness—good, bad, and everything in between.

Be present

An essential part of the curative process involves creating an experience in which your client feels "seen" and understood in his suffering. This is what will happen when, under your guidance and in your presence, he revisits the old conflict with new insight, and connects his emotional reaction to the event.

A central need in everyone's life is to be truly seen by others—to be valued and understood and listened to. Many people do not have this experience. They often experience their loved ones as not listening to them, not really understanding how they are being affected by their relationship or by a difficult situation, not hearing what their needs and wishes are. We've explored this dynamic in Chapter Four, "When Safety, Self-Worth, and Boundaries Are Violated," in our discussion of emotional neglect. Sadly, it's a common dynamic in far too many relationships, and a reason too many people lack the support they need to face the difficult emotions that arise in response to life's various challenges.

It's also why the therapeutic relationship is so powerful and so healing, because at last—perhaps for the first time in her life—your client has an opportunity to experience what it's like to be truly listened to, to talk with someone who is truly present. It's that compassionate presence that will give her the courage she needs to explore and heal unresolved losses.

Maintain healthy boundaries

The therapeutic relationship is an intimate one. Your client will share things with you that she may never share with anyone else. That's as it should be, as it needs to be. However, among the things that make it safe for her to do so are the clear, healthy boundaries you'll establish and maintain. Unlike the co-dependent or enmeshed relationships she may have experienced in her personal life, it's essential that she knows there's a place where she ends and you begin. While you've come together for the common goal of healing her unresolved losses, her needs are her needs and yours are yours. Her time and schedule are hers and yours are yours—you share an agreed upon amount of time with her each week, but she does not have unlimited access to your time. Similarly, her emotions are hers and yours are yours. She can feel free to share her most painful emotions with you *only* if she can trust that you won't be consumed by them. That's why boundaries are so important.

Here are some of the things you can do to set and maintain healthy boundaries—and what's at risk if you don't:

- Have a set time to begin and end your sessions. Letting a client have ten extra minutes may feel nice, but it's not therapeutic. When you take care of your time, it lets her know you'll take care of yourself in the face of her big feelings and big stories. It's a little like raising a child. The child needs to know what the rules are and how far she can push, so she feels safe. She can still explore her own thoughts and feelings and test the parent, but feels reassured that the parent is in charge and will ultimately take care of her. The same is true of your client. If she sees that you will take care of yourself, she's reassured that you will take care of her, too. If, on the other hand, you give your client extra time whenever she wants it, she will sense that you are not containing her, and she will begin to feel unsafe.

- Establish a cancellation policy that works for you, let your client know what it is, and stick to it. Your client may ask for special treatment—after all, she wants to feel that she's special to you. It might feel good to both of you to give her what she wants. However, in the long run, I believe she will become angry when she senses that you're not taking care of yourself, that the rules are changing, that she no longer feels safe. Of course, I'm not talking about rigidity here. There are circumstances in which compromise and understanding are called for. But those should be the exception.

- Be cautious about self-disclosure. Keep in mind that your client will project her unresolved losses from personal relationships onto you. If she becomes too involved in your personal life, those projections can become all the more deep-seated and complex—and more difficult to untangle. Also, a central tenet of psychotherapy is that we help our clients find out about themselves—who they are, what they like and dislike, what their dreams are for themselves, what their opinions are, and so forth. When we as therapists disclose our personal feelings, experiences, and beliefs, we are at risk of circumventing clients' self-exploration. They may feel inhibited about sharing their own views for fear of disappointing us or making us angry, or out of fear that we will no longer like them. There is no rulebook about what to share and what not to share. Be mindful of the issues at hand, then use your good judgment and common sense.

Ultimately, the best way to create healthy boundaries with your clients is to know what yours are. This is one of the reasons it is imperative that you enter therapy yourself, if you have not already done so. It is also important to continue to have ongoing consultations throughout your career, with either a peer group or a paid consultant. A good therapy experience will teach you a great deal of valuable information about the process. You will learn what it feels like to share the unspeakable with a stranger, and what it takes to establish trust with a therapist—and why healthy boundaries are essential to establishing trust. (See Chapter Nine, "A Therapist's Blind Spots," for a more thorough discussion.)

The Therapeutic Process

There's a reason why your client picked up the phone, made the first appointment, and brought herself to your office. Something was bothering her. Naturally, you'll need to get the full story about that difficulty as a starting point for your work together. But as we've seen, that may be just the tip of the iceberg.

Taking a history

Many pages of this book have been devoted to discussion of childhood experiences, present-day relationships, the way a client functions in her work—because those are some of the places we find information about the losses that are at the heart of the difficulty that brought her to treatment. All of these things together make up your client's personal history. It's all information that can help you to understand what losses she's endured and how she's endured them. The easiest way to get this information is to ask. For detailed guidelines regarding the kinds of information you'll need to gather, refer to Chapter Three, "Unearthing Past Experiences of Loss." Having a complete history will be invaluable as you navigate the complicated path to the real truth behind your client's difficulties.

However, the pace at which you gather information is different for every therapist and for every client. The more information you have early on, the sooner you'll have a sense of how to guide the process. But it's not reasonable to expect to get all the information in the first session, or even in the second or third. In fact, it may be threatening to your client if you try. Finding the right balance is a skill you'll develop and refine as you gain experience, and throughout your career.

I like to begin taking a history in my early sessions with a new client. However, I don't usually ask a lot of questions when we first meet. I like to use the first hour to help her get a sense of how I work, to find out what brings her to therapy, and to find out how I can be of help to her. I have found that clients will often mention painful issues in the first hour, and then not bring them up again until they feel more comfortable and safe in therapy. So taking careful notes from the start about what they say, and the more subtle cues I observe, can be a source of clues I may not get again for a while.

The second session is when I usually invite a new client to let me take a history. However, I never insist on it, because at that point I still don't know who she is regarding her need for privacy, control, and self-regulation. This is one of many areas where, as a therapist, you'll need to use your intuition to evaluate what is going on between you and your client.

Keep in mind that one of your highest priorities is to establish trust, and take care not to press for information if it feels like an intrusion or a violation to her, especially at the beginning of your relationship. It can easily feel overwhelming to be asked for information she might not be ready to share. It's essential that you focus early on—beginning in that very first meeting—on understanding who this individual is, her emotional awareness, and how she relates to you. You'll want her to be as comfortable as possible; be mindful of the insecurity or anxiety she might be feeling. Remember: She may never really have talked directly with someone…sitting quietly in a room, making eye contact and showing real interest in her…until now.

Identifying key experiences of loss

It's possible your client has entered therapy because he's decided to address the central issue of loss that has haunted him his entire life. More often, though, by far, there are several experiences of loss that lie buried many layers beneath the surface, creating a complex of repressed emotions and conflicts. Chances are the problem that brought your client to see you is really just a symptom of the many losses he's endured. It's your job to help him peel away the many layers to find the losses that continue to cause him pain, decipher his coping strategies—some of which may have been in place for decades—and help him learn new ways of resolving the old issues of loss and the new ones that will inevitably come his way.

Refer often to the lists of symptoms related to the various types of loss in Part Two, "Your Client's Experience," in this book. They'll help you to be attuned to the kinds of coping mechanisms that often accompany each loss, and point you to likely areas of concern.

Identifying the losses that remain unresolved requires your best powers of observation and deduction. You'll need to:

- ask questions…lots and lots of questions;
- pay attention to the content of his stories, listening for any recurring themes of conflict;
- find out what story he has told himself about his childhood;
- observe what story he tells himself about who he is today;
- take note of his behavior when he speaks about a particular event or issue—his mannerisms, speech patterns, resistance;
- evaluate depressive symptoms such as weight gain or loss, sleep disorder, or emotional withdrawal;

- listen, listen, listen. People tell you what is important if you listen closely.

Remember that most people have been taught not to express difficult emotions or talk about messy problems. It's up to you to ask what might appear to be the obvious questions—don't assume he'll volunteer everything there is to say about the matter. Asking probing questions is essential to helping him to talk further about uncomfortable issues and to move beyond his notions about what is and is not okay to talk about.

When he does begin to share the tough stuff it's important to be as non-judgmental as possible—of your client as well as the people who treated him badly—and not to overreact to the stories, situations, and atrocities you will hear about. Your client will be very keen on observing you and aware of your discomfort, which he may translate as a message to stop talking. I'm not suggesting you be dishonest or non-emotional. Let him see your compassion and empathy, but moderate any emotional response you may have. You'll want your client to have big feelings, and not have them overshadowed by your reaction.

Resolution and healing: Grieving the loss

When we understand that there is an element of loss at the heart of every trauma, it becomes clear that grief plays a pivotal role in resolving and healing those traumas. Why is grief so important? When emotional trauma occurs something precious has been taken away—hence the element of loss. The grief that ensues can be excruciating to the point of being debilitating, and we often go to great lengths to avoid it. But in the truest sense, grief *is* healing. Until we grieve our losses we cannot let them go, and they continue to haunt us and color every aspect of our lives.

The five stages of grief

In 1969 Swiss psychiatrist Elisabeth Kübler-Ross published the seminal book *On Death and Dying*, in which she identified five stages of grief: denial, anger, bargaining, depression, and acceptance. These are the stages each of us must go through as we come to terms with loss. While her work was initially related to grieving related to death, we now know that the same process applies to grief related to any loss. Dr. Kübler-Ross's analysis was so powerful, and her insights so valuable, that they remain foundational to any study of the grieving process. Understanding the process in this way will enable you to guide your clients through their own grief processes toward successful outcomes.

The five stages of grief as defined by Dr. Kübler-Ross are as follows:

- **Denial.** At first we tend to deny the loss has taken place because it is too overwhelming. We pretend it's not true or, if it is, it's not as bad as all that. We try to convince ourselves we can avoid it, or that it will just go away. Or we may simply be in shock.
- **Anger.** We may be furious at the person who inflicted the hurt, or angry at the world for letting it happen. We might be angry with ourselves for allowing the event to occur, even though realistically nothing could

have stopped it. We might even be angry at God for not taking better care of us.

- **Bargaining.** Some people try to make a deal with God, asking, "If I do this, will you take away the loss?" Others engage in behaviors or adopt remedies in hopes that doing so will make the trouble go away. There's a desperate hope that something, somehow, some way will allow them to avoid facing the loss as it is.

- **Depression.** In this stage numbness often sets in. We withdraw into ourselves, unable to face our pain or completely overwhelmed by it. A sense of hopelessness is common, as it seems impossible to carry on in the face of such a terrible loss.

- **Acceptance.** This is when we begin to find resolution, as we accept the reality of the loss. At last we recognize that life will in fact go on, and that we may in fact be able to endure the loss after all.

A few people move through these stages one after another, from start to finish. For the vast majority, though, the grieving process is not linear. Your client may move forward and back within the stages, or move through them in a different order. He might get stuck in a particular stage, so that you'll need to go deeper into your work until he feels safe and ready to move ahead.

What's clear is that each client will move through the grieving process in his own unique way. As with any other aspect of treatment, plan to treat each client as an individual, follow his lead, and be prepared to support him according to his particular needs. A successful resolution of loss will not be based on "getting through the stages" as much as coming to terms with the loss, accepting it, and reclaiming the sense of self.

Making the connection

Remember that loss begets loss. When your client has difficulty accepting a recent loss, chances are there are older, similar losses that remain unresolved. A client named Sharon had started a new relationship, and quickly began to worry that her new partner would leave her without warning. I remembered that her grandmother had died suddenly of a heart attack, with no opportunity to say goodbye. When I pointed out that the loss of her grandmother might be surfacing in her fears about her new relationship, Sharon was able to understand the connection and release her fears about her new love leaving her.

And so, the upside of "loss begets loss" is that healing old loss begets healing current ills. In simple terms, help your client connect the dots in the context of the healing process, and the domino effect will work to her advantage.

When Your Work Is Done

Is the work of therapy ever done? No, it's not. Healing is a process...a never ending process. It teaches your client not to be afraid to know the truth about himself and his life, and offers coping strategies for life and love and sorrow and conflict. As a result of your work together he'll learn to reconnect with his emotional self and to feel comfortable experiencing and expressing it. Mastering those skills will be part of a lifelong endeavor.

When is it time to let go?

When your client is living in his authentic best self he is able to share friendliness, warmth, humor, sincerity, energy, interest, enthusiasm, and love. He feels free and safe enough to depend on others as well as himself. When he understands himself deeply and honestly he can change the way he relates to others and to himself, and can handle distressing situations with grace. On the job he works toward meaningful accomplishments that are in line with his deepest values. When your client has the knowledge and wisdom to create the life he envisions and the ability to reach his fullest potential, he has received what he needs from therapy, and it's your job to help him know it is time to say goodbye and "leave home."

Most of us did not have the opportunity to say goodbye to our parents when we left home. In fact, many people haven't really left home, even though they no longer live in the same house as their parents. One of the most difficult things for many people to overcome is the struggle to move beyond their parents. If Mom or Dad has difficulty letting go, grown-up children often don't break the bonds out of a sense of guilt or obligation. Once again, your therapeutic relationship with your client will model a healthier process.

When you near the end of your work together, closure becomes an important part of bringing treatment to completion. As a therapist you become a surrogate parent for your client, so helping him say goodbye to you is like reenacting leaving home in a healthy way. Whereas his parents may have wanted to hold on to him forever, it is important for you to make it clear that he has permission to get well, attain emotional health, and say goodbye to you. If the two of you have done good work, he will be living a life he only dreamed possible, one that is enriched with more opportunity and knowledge than he could attain before therapy. The final element of healing you can offer is to be sure he realizes that leaving a parent—or surrogate parent—behind is not a betrayal, but a happy, healthy, necessary event. While his parents may not have been capable of doing so, you can encourage him to pursue his dreams, join him in his dreams, and, yes…*help him grieve his loss of you!*

CHAPTER NINE

A Therapist's Blind Spots

In an ideal world, a therapist will have sorted out her own emotional challenges and difficulties before embarking on a career healing others. She'll know how to set clear boundaries in her personal, professional, and therapeutic relationships, and have resolved all her old issues of loss so that there are no repressed emotions to distort her interactions with others. She'll be adept at noticing her emotions as they arise, all of which will be reasonable and direct responses to events in the present moment.

All of that may be ideal, but it's not realistic. The truth is that few human beings possess that level of clarity, or are that free of lingering impact from the losses of their past. As we've acknowledged in previous chapters, all of us—including therapists—have experienced loss, and the impact of those losses affects our relationships—including therapeutic relationships. It's not reasonable to expect that you'll be completely free of the influence of the losses in your history when you step inside your office.

What *is* reasonable is to make it a priority to become knowledgeable about where your potential blind spots are, the areas where an old loss might interfere with your ability to respond to your client solely on the basis of what he brings to the table—not what you have lurking in your unconscious.

Transference and countertransference

One of the reasons the therapeutic relationship creates a context for healing is that it's an opportunity for a client to explore the dynamics of problematic relationships. Some of that work happens when a client projects the thoughts, feelings, or behavior of someone else onto the therapist. For example, if his mother was overly critical he might see your questions as badgering, and believe that he hears judgment in your voice even when you're feeling completely accepting and compassionate toward him. His perception has nothing to do with your behavior, and everything to do with his projections. This dynamic is called "transference," and is a normal component of therapy. When your client's old reactions to his mother resurface in the safety of his work with you, the two of you can explore those reactions so that he gains awareness and understanding of them. He'll also gain valuable insight into how he experiences himself and how he experiences you. As you explore his transference and his unresolved losses, while holding the boundaries and frame of the therapeutic relationship, you'll establish a secure environment in which your client can express all of his feelings—including sexual ones—and trust that you will not act out against him.

When a similar dynamic occurs in reverse, we call it "countertransference." Simply stated, countertransference is any reaction you have to a client that is determined by *your own* life history and unconscious content. For example, there will be times when a client begins to represent for you someone from your past with whom you have unresolved or unmet feelings, needs, or desires. If you begin to project those feelings, needs, or desires onto your client, that's countertransference. When this occurs, it's often marked by a strong emotional reaction, such as anger, repulsion, or sexual feelings. Many of those feelings will be primarily about your own history of unresolved losses, but they can also provide clues to your client's psychology—they may be a direct response to his transference. The key for you is to distinguish which reactions are about you and which ones are about him. If you allow your own projections to go on unchecked, and you get lost in your own reactivity, it becomes extremely difficult for you to maintain clarity about your client's issues, emotions, and reactions, and impossible for you to be an effective therapist.

However, if you are mindful of the dynamics of countertransference it can provide valuable information regarding your relationship with your client, because it essentially mirrors what's going on for him. When you find yourself projecting the thoughts, feelings, or behaviors of someone else onto your client, chances are it's because *his* deeper issues of loss have been triggered.

When you become aware of the process as it emerges, you can then proceed to explore those issues with him.

What are the signs that countertransference may be peeking over your shoulder, in spite of your best efforts to avoid it?

- You notice that something about your client diminishes your objectivity.
- You have an inappropriate reaction, such as a negative judgment, disbelief, or erotic or hostile feelings toward him, something that strikes a familiar note in relation to your own history.
- You find yourself distracted, or have difficulty focusing on what your client is saying.
- He reminds you of your parent, sibling, partner, friend, or teacher.
- You find yourself wanting to "fix him," or having difficulty letting him go.
- You notice you've revealed more about your personal life than is appropriate.
- Some therapists even become involved in a romantic relationship with clients because of countertransference.

The key to using countertransference as a valuable professional tool—rather than allowing it to cloud your judgment and interfere with your work—is awareness, awareness, and awareness.

- Do everything in your power to be aware of your own issues of loss, and any unresolved emotions you still carry.

- Be astutely aware of any emotions, judgments, or other reactions that arise as you work with a client, and be on the lookout for times when your own issues might be entering the picture. Notice how your body feels (relaxed or tense, hot or cold; how you're breathing), and what you think or feel when you look at your client. Monitor any fantasies that come to mind, who he reminds you of, what you like or don't like about him.

- Be aware of what you must do to constructively use your countertransference when it does arise. Recognize the underlying message that your client is experiencing transference, and help him gain his own new awareness.

The best, most essential tool at your disposal to develop your awareness in all these areas is therapy—for you. It's the best path to resolving your own issues of loss, and will also give you the skills you need to monitor your reactions as they emerge while treating clients.

If you haven't already done extensive therapy, I urge you to do it now. Today. Put this book down, pick up the phone, get some referrals, and make an appointment. Until you've done a thorough exploration of your own issues of loss, you can't possibly know when they're invading your relationships with your clients.

Once you've done—or are doing—your own inner work, meet regularly with a peer group or a consultant who will help you explore the countertransference arising in your work, as well as the areas of loss you're still working on. On your own, even in the best of circumstances, it can be difficult to discern whether you're having a legitimate reaction to a client or dealing with countertransference. Meeting regularly with colleagues who face the same issues in their work is a valuable resource for maintaining the clarity you need. A consultant can also provide that service for you. And of course, be sure to make it a practice to keep up with your professional reading and attend workshops and trainings on a regular basis.

The superhero

Be wary of expecting too much of yourself. Know where you excel, and also know your limitations. It's great to feel confident about the skills, talents, and personal qualities you bring to your work as a healer. It's also great—and necessary—to recognize that there are areas you're still working on, and that potentially pose liabilities in your ability to be effective. It's not possible to be outstanding in every aspect of your work. Your life history, your unique way of interacting with people, your values and priorities, and any number of other attributes will serve you well in some circumstances, but may be less helpful in others.

For instance, if you are yourself a survivor of abuse or neglect (as many therapists are), it can be a great source of understanding, skills, and experience as you work with clients struggling with a similar history. But you also need to be sure you feel in a strong enough place at this point in time, and that you have the support you need, to do the stressful work of helping a client face the same demons that will tap you on the shoulder every now and then for the rest of your life. If you ignore the reality of your own limitations, you run the risk of trying to resolve unaddressed issues of your own through your clients. However, if you can be starkly honest with yourself about what you can and cannot do, you'll be in a better position to turn your liabilities into assets, so that both you and your clients emerge as winners.

Infallibility

Sometimes it's a matter of ego; more often it springs from a deep and sincere desire to be everything a client needs in a therapist. Whatever the cause, too often healing professionals believe they are—or should be—infallible. If you set perfection as your only measure of success, failure is the only option and everyone will suffer, including your clients. If you feel a need to *appear* infallible to your clients, you're also setting yourself up for failure. Most clients have of necessity learned to be astute observers of human nature, and they can usually spot a lack of authenticity.

You are going to make mistakes. You'll miss an important cue from a client, make a comment you'll wish you hadn't, or succumb for a moment to the murky web of countertransference. When it happens, you must first accept it as a sign you're human (thank goodness!), and then forgive yourself. Just as important, acknowledge your error to your client. You don't need to share why you faltered, or any personal history behind it. But it's important to be honest, and to reassure her that it was not her fault. Saying "I'm sorry" is therapeutic for both of you, and provides a good model of responsibility and honesty for her.

Chapter Ten

Healing the Healer

I trust that if you are reading this book you are already on the path of healing yourself, living the life you want, and ready to help others on their journeys. It is my hope that as you read this book, in addition to gaining insights about treating your clients, you also awakened memories and connections that stirred some unconscious part of you, and that this new awareness will move you into a deeper understanding of yourself. That, in turn, will allow you to help your clients do the same thing. As the old expression goes, "Healer, heal thyself." We are only available to heal our clients when we have undertaken the journey to heal our own lives.

There is no all-encompassing cure for the human condition with its inherent trials and tribulations. No one can put an end to emotional trauma, addiction, depression, or any other difficult human experience once and for all.

You can't control what has happened in your life or what will happen. What you do have control over is how you relate to it. You can choose to find solutions for the difficulties that arise as a result of your challenges, and seek recovery from your suffering. Once you make that choice, you have the capacity to heal yourself and live a full and happy life.

How Do We Heal?

When I think about healing, the following words come to mind:

- Fearlessness
- Perseverance
- Patience
- Trust
- Faith
- Commitment
- Gratitude
- Mindfulness
- And love…always love

We all need to become fearless in our search for the truth about our lives—but that's especially true for those of us who assume the honor and the responsibility of helping others in their quest for truth. As we discussed in Chapter Nine, "A Therapist's Blind Spots," if you are unaware of the losses that have impacted your own life, they're likely to be triggered by the work you do with your clients—to no one's benefit. The more whole and healthy you are, the better you'll be able to guide those who come to you for help in their search for truth.

This book is about living with and accepting the knowledge that we have all suffered losses, and that too often we move on with our lives without ever acknowledging them or the pain we experience as a result. Those unnamed traumas and feelings are buried deep in our unconscious minds. That's true for you, just as it is for every client who walks in your door. Becoming aware of your own losses and accepting them is the first and most important step on your own journey toward the healing that is necessary if you are to live authentically…if you are to be truly alive…and if you are to realize your true gifts as a healer.

I have spoken about patterns that develop early in our lives that shape the way we receive, think about, and experience the world and ourselves. Those patterns are based on beliefs that are deeply rooted—beliefs about ourselves, the significant others in our lives, and the ways we relate to them and to the world. We get attached to beliefs when we are growing up, and sadly many of those beliefs have little to do with the reality of our lives. We usually adopt our parents' beliefs, and don't question many of them as we become adults. We do this, in part, so we can feel that we belong to our families, and so that, by agreeing with them, we can continue to feel close to them. In truth, what we really want from them is emotional closeness, openness, and honesty. The artificial closeness we feel when we pretend to agree, at the expense of our own authenticity, only perpetuates the emptiness and loneliness we feel inside.

It is challenging to give up those beliefs, even though what we adopt in their place is far more satisfying. Change can be frightening, especially when it involves something as fundamental as our beliefs about who we are. But as you know, when you face your fears you overcome them. Most of the fears you live with today originated in experiences from your early life. If you don't work them out, they will stay with you, living in you as if they were actually happening today. They become the filter you use to gauge what is safe, real, and possible to have and achieve in your life today. And they color your perceptions as you strive to understand the client who sits before you.

When you become more adept at acknowledging, experiencing, and expressing your emotions you deepen your connection to who you really are. As the process evolves and you rethink your beliefs about who you are, where you came from, and what you can hope for in this life, your ability to be present and available to your clients will also deepen. You will have a greater understanding of her struggles and more clarity about the way she relates to you and everyone else in her life.

This book has been an exploration of loss as an inevitable part of the human condition, and why it's so necessary to address it, heal it, and resolve it. Each of us owes it to ourselves to resolve the losses that have come our way. As a therapist, the gifts that come from your own healing will have a ripple effect on the lives of those you heal. As you reclaim your true emotions and beliefs you will begin to forge new relationships in your personal life and as a professional, based on your new authenticity. If family members are able to grow with you and accept your newfound awareness, your relationships with them will deepen. If not, you must seek support and connection with friends and colleagues who are on a similar journey, and create a "family of choice" that provides the closeness, openness, and honesty you crave. In that context you will find the relationships that will support you on your lifelong healing journey.

As you learn to identify your strengths, focus on them, and use them to help you enrich your own life, they will also become great assets in your arsenal of tools for healing your clients. Although none of us can stop loss from happening, you can be in charge of how you live with it, and be a model for how your clients can live with theirs.

You are already well on your way in your journey to heal your own losses. That's the best, most important step in becoming an effective healer for your clients. Knowing how to do that is, after all, what every therapist needs to know.

About the Author

Ginny Pizzardi, M.S., M.F.T., has been a practicing psychotherapist since 1985. Over the years she has counseled hundreds of people struggling to resolve difficult issues, often involving personal loss. Her early professional experience dealt largely with families and survivors of family violence, abuse, addiction, and adoption. In listening to and counseling her clients, she discovered lessons in loss that could be useful to others in helping professions. Extensive professional training coupled with her own life experience gave Ginny a wealth of real-life perspectives on the special challenges of loss. Over time she was inspired to share this knowledge with her fellow therapists, which she now does through this book, as a speaker and teacher, and in private consultations.

One of her goals for *Lessons in Loss* is to shed light on why people continue to struggle even though they have received counseling and therapy. The truth is that many clients never really go through the grief process to final resolution. This guide was written to help therapists and their clients make the journey complete.

Ginny offers workshops and consultation for therapists who wish to expand their understanding of loss and the impact it has on the lives of their clients. She continues to work as a psychotherapist in private practice in San Francisco, California, and is currently an Analytic Candidate in training at the Psychoanalytic Institute of Northern California. Her website address is www.GinnyPizzardi.com.